/M/ AMERICAN **MARKETING** ASSOCIATION

# AMA HANDBOOK FOR

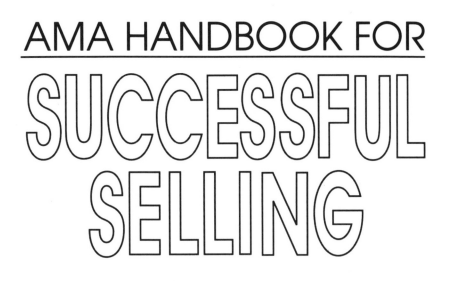

SUCCESSFUL SELLING

## BOB KIMBALL
University of West Florida

American Marketing Association
Chicago, Illinois

NTC Business Books
*NTC/Contemporary Publishing Group*

**Library of Congress Cataloging-in-Publication Data**

Kimball, Bob.
     AMA handbook for successful selling / Bob Kimball.
       p.   cm.
     ISBN 0-8442-3588-1 (Hardbound)
     ISBN 0-8442-3591-1 (Softbound)
     1. Selling.   I. Title.
     HF5438.25.K546
     658.8'5—dc20                  93-2784
                                       CIP

Published in conjunction with the American Marketing Association,
250 South Wacker Drive, Chicago, Illinois 60606

Published by NTC Business Books
A division of NTC/Contemporary Publishing Group, Inc.
4255 West Touhy Avenue, Lincolnwood (Chicago), Illinois 60646-1975 U.S.A.
Printed in the United States of America
International Standard Book Number: 0-8442-3588-1 (cloth)
                                      0-8442-3591-1 (paper)
18   17   16   15   14   13   12   11   10   9   8   7   6   5

# Contents

———

## Chapter 4    Identifying and Developing Prospects    71
The Five Top Secrets of Prospecting and Preparation

## Chapter 5    A Sales Call Is a Performance    97
The Six Top Secrets for Making Your Presentation a Winner

## Chapter 6    Enhance Your Power Position in the Selling Situation    119
The Seven Top Secrets of Power and Negotiation

# About the Author

Bob Kimball began his career in sales with the Coca-Cola Company, where, in addition to selling products and prospecting for new customers, he designed and conducted sales training programs. In 1981, he set up his own sales management/training group, The Kimball Organization, servicing a diverse range of consumer, service, and business-to-business clients. They include Coca-Cola USA, Cotton States Insurance Companies, Lanier Business Products, and Pabst Brewing Company.

Bob is currently Associate Professor at the University of West Florida, where he teaches courses in Professional Selling, Sales Management, and Distribution Management. He received his PhD and also taught at the University of Georgia. A recipient of numerous awards for teaching excellence, his articles have been published in such publications as *Marketing News*, *The Journal of Marketing Education*, and *The Journal of Consumer Marketing*.

# INTRODUCTION

# What This Book Is About

This book is about selling and what it takes to become a professional salesperson. The key word here is *professional*. Think about it for a moment. When you hear the word professional, what comes to mind? Doctor? Lawyer? Professor? Business executive? Probably not salesperson.

What image does come to mind when you hear the word salesperson? Some guy in a checkered sport coat and loud tie trying to peddle a used car that a little old lady drove only to church on Sundays and to bingo on Wednesday nights? A housewife who dabbles in real estate on weekends to make a little extra spending money? A fast-talking insurance salesman you do your best to avoid? Probably nothing you would consider professional.

How much prestige is associated with being a salesperson? Prestige? Are you kidding? If you're in sales now, I'll bet you can remember the reaction you got from friends and family when you first told them you were accepting a position as a salesperson. Ooo's and Ah's? I doubt it. Probably something more along the line of: "Why would you want to do that?" or "Don't you think you're good enough to get a *real* job?" If they didn't say that to you personally, chances are pretty good they made those comments to each other when your name came up at a time when you weren't around.

Perhaps you do a lot of traveling. I'd hate to try to count how many of the best years of my life have been spent at the gate waiting for airplanes. But whether it's there or any other place where strangers congregate, after introducing yourselves to each other, what's the first question to come up? Of course! "What do you do for a living?" Tell them you're a college professor or a writer and there's an instant rapport. Tell them you're in sales and it's an automatic "Excuse me." In fact, you may have discovered, as I have, that one of the easiest ways to get ride of someone you don't want to deal with is to tell them you're in sales. Cemetery plots are particularly effective.

Maybe one or both of your parents were in sales. My dad was. I can still remember as a little kid when I'd be out playing with all the other children in the neighborhood and one of them would start in with the "What does your daddy do?" game. Sound familiar?

"Hey, Johnny, what does your daddy do?"

And Johnny would put his thumbs inside his belt, strut around for a few steps, and say: "My daddy works for the govva-mint!"

"Ooooo!"

"Wow!"

"Man!"

Then it was: "Hey, Suzie, what does *your* daddy do?"

And Suzie would look up, her eyes twinkling and her face beaming, and say: "My daddy, he's an enja-neer!"

"Gee!"

"Hey!"

"Neat-o!"

I knew it was coming, and it finally did: "Hey, skinny Bobby Kimball, what does *your* daddy do?"

And my shoulders would slump, my head would drop, and my eyes would stare vacantly at the ground.

"M-m-m-my daddy. . . H-h-he's just a s-s-s-salesman."

Why is this so? What's going on? Why the bad rap for the selling profession? Let's think about it for a moment.

First of all, what does it take to call oneself a salesperson? To the best of my knowledge, there are no PhD's in salesmanship. Many colleges and universities offer courses in selling, but few, if any, offer a masters in salesmanship or an undergraduate major in selling. I've never heard of any licensing standards which must be met, nor of any boards of accreditation that certify people worthy of practicing sales. In fact, I'll bet that if you put this book down right now and went out knocking on the doors of businesses, within 24 hours you'd have a job as a salesperson. To be sure, you might be on straight commission with no salary, draw, or expense account. And you'd have to write in your name on the business cards. But you'd be able to say that you were employed as a salesperson.

Here's the point: *Anyone* can say they're in sales. But there's a whole world of difference between being in sales and being a *professional salesperson*. My dad is a professional salesperson. I pride myself in being a professional salesperson. That's what this book is all about.

Consider this: Maybe you've never thought of it this way, but even if you're not employed in a sales position, you *are* a salesperson. For better or for worse, you're selling every day. If you're in a staff support position, you may have ideas and programs which you hope to convince management to adopt. That's salesmanship. Or you're dreaming about a fishing trip to the mountains for your vacation this year and need your family's enthusiasm and support. *That's* salesmanship. Perhaps you want your teenager to spend less time watching TV and more time studying. Salesmanship! Or maybe you're trying to get someone to hire you, or you've just met someone you desire to have like you and want to spend time with you. *Salesmanship*, with you as the product. You can't escape this simple fact: Like it or not, day in and day out, you *are* a salesperson. You may be a very effective salesperson or a profoundly ineffective one, but you *are* a salesperson. And since being an *effective* and *professional* salesperson can help you have more and be more—to be richer *and* happier—there's just no other way to go, is there?

If you're interested in becoming a professional salesperson, this book is for you. First, you'll learn what professional selling is. Then you'll analyze those personal qualities which are the foundation of success. Finally, you'll learn the requisite skills necessary to make things happen. So turn the page and let's get started.

# CHAPTER 1

# What Is Professional Salesmanship?

---

## The Seven Top Secrets of Professionalism

Let's face it, to the average person, the term salesperson does not imply professional. The stereotypical salesperson is someone to be avoided, not a person you would respect and trust as a consultant and partner. So, the first thing we need to understand is what it means and what it takes to be a *professional* salesperson.

In this chapter we'll look at the Seven Top Secrets of Professionalism, those things that make the difference between being "just a salesperson" and being an effective professional salesperson. The very first secret is that salesmanship is not a talent but a learned skill. Working hard and doing the right things are the keys to success. And nothing is more important than attaining expert knowledge about every aspect of your profession.

Another secret of professional salespeople is that they listen more than they speak. That's how they discover the benefits their prospects want and need. They put themselves in the customer's shoes and help them buy, building value rather than just lowering price. Let's take a look at each of these seven secrets one at a time.

# Secret 1:
# Salesmanship Is a Skill, Not a Talent

We all admire gifted people. There's nothing quite like a Ted Williams swing, an Emmitt Smith run, a Gary Larson cartoon. Sure, they had to work and sacrifice to achieve their peak potential, but the gift was there. I've often wondered what it would be like to play ball in the major leagues: Center-fielder for the Cubs, leading them to six consecutive world championships. How about that? If I'd started at four years old, working out and practicing every day, could I have made that dream come true? What do you think? Could I have done it? Yes? What? Get serious! I have no natural athletic ability whatsoever! I make a brontosaurus look like a ballerina! I guess if I'd given baseball my total dedication from the age of four, I might have played at the collegiate level at a small school in a conference with a 12-game schedule. But major league? I just don't have the talent. That's all there is to it. Some got it, some don't.

People often make the mistake of comparing sports and salesmanship. They talk of a "natural" salesperson, a "born" salesperson, and the like.

But salesmanship is a skill, not a natural gift. When a person has mastered a skill, it *seems* easy and natural. The guy who works on my car effortlessly diagnoses and rectifies problems which would confound less experienced mechanics. It looks natural, but I know it's the result of many years' knowledge, learned skills, and practice. The same can be said for everything from brain surgery to plumbing. When you watch a true professional at work, it looks easy. I've never attempted brain surgery, but I have tried my hand at plumbing. After killing an entire day under the kitchen sink, interspersed with half a dozen trips to and from the hardware store, I gave it up and called the plumber. Twenty minutes and a $50 service charge later, all was well. Mechanics, surgeons, plumbers. In these professions we all know there are specific skills, learned over time, which enable a person to perform effectively and seemingly effortlessly. Yet in salesmanship, we somehow think the skills are more inherent than learned. Let's kill that myth up front. Forget about the so-called "born salesperson." Professional salesmanship is a *learned* skill. Not somewhat learned. Not mostly learned. *Learned*, period! You, me, *anyone* can learn that skill. Skeptical? That's understandable. You've probably been conditioned to believe you're an "OK" salesperson or a "good" salesperson, but never thought you could be one of the best. Fine. Just keep reading, learning, and developing the awareness and skills presented in this book. Yes, *skills*. This book is about learned skills, not techniques. There are lots of books about techniques. Six hundred sure-fire closing techniques! Sixty ways to turn objections into opportunities! Six hundred sixty techniques for getting the appointment! Don't get me wrong. There's nothing wrong with techniques. But techniques alone, without the commensurate skills, won't get you very far.

# Secret 2:
# Salesmanship Starts with Knowledge

Knowledge is the foundation upon which professional selling is built. Building a sale is no different than building a house. Skimp on the foundation, cut a corner here, cut a corner there, and the house falls down.

As a professional salesperson, you've got to know everything there is to know about:

**(1) Your Product or Service**    You've got to be an expert. How and where is it made? Do you know all the technical specifications and whether they meet the customer's requirements? What are the product's features and applications, and what *benefits* can they provide your customers? How about your pricing and billing procedures? What kinds of warranty and service support does your company provide? Are you fully familiar with your product's performance compared with competitors? What experiences have customers had with your product? Are you current on all your company's advertisements and publications? And is there anything you can learn from the experiences of your boss, your fellow salespeople, and others?

Product knowledge is just one corner of the foundation. It's very important, but it can't stand alone. Product knowledge won't help you without similar knowledge about:

**(2) Your Customers and Their Needs**    When it comes to your customers, you should know more about them than they know about themselves. That's the secret to consultive selling, where you act not only as a supplier of products or services, but also as a trusted consultant and advisor. The professional salesperson doesn't just sell products. He or she brings to each client business-building ideas and solutions to problems. For the customer, consulting with a professional salesperson is like having another vital person on the team at no cost. How's *your* customer knowledge and how well do you know *all* the key people in their customer's organization? That's right: *All* the key people. Often, salespeople make the mistake of focusing their attention narrowly on the so-called "decision maker." Sure, that's the person you have to get to because he or she has the final say and releases the dollars to buy. But don't miss opportunities for information and insights you could get by developing relationships with everyone else in the company, from the CEO to the janitor.

So you know everything there is to know about your product and your customer. Think that's enough? Not by a long shot. Find out about:

**(3) Your Competition**    Who are your competitors and what do you know about them? What are their products or services like and how do they compare to yours? For every element of knowledge you have about your company and its products, you need to have similar knowledge about the competition. Know their advantages and disadvantages. Know your strengths. Acknowledge your limitations. And in light of all this, develop the strategy and tactics that give you the greatest probability of winning.

Finally, you've got to know:

**(4) Your Industry**  This means keeping up with all your industry and trade associations and getting exposure for yourself and your company in the industry and trade journals. Keep track of legislation and regulation, be aware of product alternatives and innovations from domestic and foreign competition, and have a feel for economic and financial conditions that may impact your industry.

You've got to know it all: Product, customer, competition, and industry! Think that means a lot of hard work and study? You bet! But what's the alternative? Can you afford to make a sales call knowing less than all you can know? Of course not. Remember what you just read about professional selling being a learned skill? Learning starts with knowledge, so get to work!

# Secret 3: Remember the Magic Word—Listen

Recently, I witnessed—eavesdropped on—an intriguing encounter between an apparently struggling salesperson and a potential customer. I was in a hotel lobby and a dapper youngish gentleman, dressed in slacks, shirt open at the collar, and a sport coat, had just checked in. Another young man, in suit and tie, approached him. Their conversation went something like this...

| | |
|---|---|
| Salesman: | "Excuse me, sir..." |
| Prospect: | "Huh? Who are you?" |
| Salesman: | "My name is Ben Dover..." |
| Prospect: | "What are you? Some kind of weirdo?" |
| Salesman: | "Oh, no, sir, not at all. I represent the Acme Tie Company." |

Prospect:    "The what?"

Salesman:    "The Acme Tie Company. I couldn't help but notice you're not wearing a tie."

Prospect:    "You got that right."

Salesman:    "Do you mind if I ask why?"

Prospect:    "Not at all. I hate the things!"

The salesman pulled a sample out of his case.

Salesman:    "I have one here which would go just right with that outfit you're wearing."

Prospect:    "Might be, but I don't need it. Must have 50 of 'em at home. See, I'm not from here, at least not yet. My company's transferring me down, so I'm just in househunting for the weekend. Don't need a tie to go househunting."

Salesman:    "Well, let me be the first to welcome you to the area. Where are you coming from?"

Prospect:    "Athens, Georgia. Home of the Dawgs. Best party town in the world."

Salesman:    "Really?"

Prospect:    "You gotcha. The minute I set foot out of the office, it's off with the tie and into the Levi's and a T-shirt and I'm on my way to happy hour for a couple of pitchers before I go out for the evening."

Salesman:    "Sounds interesting. But getting back to the tie…"

Prospect:    "Nah, I don't think so."

Salesman:    "It's on sale this week for just twelve dollars, but today I can let you have it for ten. It goes great with your coat."

Prospect:    "No, not today. Hey, it's been great talking to you, but I've got to get up to my room. I haven't been feeling too well all day and I'm really beat. I don't understand it. I just don't hold up the way I used to. Anyhow, I've got to get me some rest. Tonight I'm going to take it easy and just sit in my room and have a nice quiet 12-pack and relax."

Salesman:    "I can't interest you in this tie, then?"
Prospect:    "Nope. See ya around. . ."

They parted. I never saw either one of them again. I often wondered about that tie salesman, though, and whether he's still in sales. If so, I'll bet he's struggling along just well enough to get by. That's because from what I could tell, he didn't know the magic word. The magic word? If there's one thing—just one thing—you remember from this book, make it the magic word. And that magic word is:

# LISTEN

Yes, listen! Too many salespeople operate under the misconception that their gift of gab will get them the sale. Nothing could be further from the truth. In fact, as a professional salesperson, your objective should be to get the customer to talk—not talk yourself. If you find you're doing more than 45 percent of the talking, it's time to do one thing: Shut up! Talk less, listen more. Because if you can get your customer to talk, he or she will tell you what you need to know to make the sale.

Let's take another look at the conversation between the tie salesman and his prospect. How long did it take? A minute, maybe a minute and a half? Not much time. But in that time, what did we learn about this potential customer?

Well, for one thing, he doesn't like ties. He has to wear them for work, and owns about 50 of them. As soon as he's out the door, though, off with the tie.

He's not from the area, and is down here to look at houses. "Don't need a tie to go househunting." By the way, did you notice how the salesman, seeing opportunity slipping away, resorted to lowering the price? A common tactic. You may have tried it a time or two yourself. But if a customer sees no need for your product, what's it worth? Right! Zilch!

What else do we know? Let's see, he's from Athens, Georgia. Loves the Dawgs. Anything more? Well, he seems to like to party. Levi's, T-shirt, and a couple of pitchers and he's ready to go out for the evening.

How's he doing today? Somewhat fatigued, it would appear. So what's he up to tonight? Going to go up to his room and get some rest, right? A little R & R and a nice quiet 12-pack.

Wow! We sure learned a lot about this guy in a minute or a minute and a half, didn't we? Now hold on. Let's get this straight. This evening, he's going to do what? Sit in his room. Relax. Quiet 12-pack. Hmm… Just a second here. Knowing what we know about this guy, what do you think is going to start going through his mind tonight, sitting in his room, somewhere around the fourth beer? You got it! Now, any ideas on how we might get this dude interested in buying a tie? Sure!

"Oh, there's no need to sit all alone in your room tonight. They've got a great little lounge right here in the hotel. Lots of people who love to party hangin' out. Bet some of them would be interested in meeting you. But just one thing. This isn't like Athens, Georgia. People around here don't go out for the evening in Levi's and a T-shirt. You gotta dress up nice. And you know what you need to be a big hit tonight?" Of course! A tie!

It's simple. Get your customers to talk. *Listen!* Find out what they really care about. Then, focus your selling effort on showing them how what you sell will help them get those things they *already* want and need. That poor tie salesman was on the wrong track trying to convince his prospect he needed a tie. Don't waste your time attempting to *create* a need. Find out what your prospect's hot button is and help him or her discover that your product will help satisfy that *existing* need.

Does everyone buy for the same reason? Does everyone have the same needs? What if the prospect had said he was a minister from Bamberg, South Carolina, away from his flock for the night, and was going to spend the evening in his room doing some inspirational reading? What would you say to him?

"Hey, man, you don't have to sit in your room doing inspirational reading. You can party 'til dawn!"

No!!! To him you'd say something like "Oh, there's no need to sit all alone in your room tonight. Why, there's a prayer meeting seven nights a week in this fair city. And you know what you need to look really sharp at that prayer meeting tonight? A tie! Yes sir, with this tie you'll look so sharp I'll bet they'll even ask you to stand up and testify!"

Let's repeat. Get the prospect to talk. *Listen!* Then point out how your product will enable your prospect to attain *existing* wants and needs.

# Secret 4:
# People Don't Buy Products— They Buy Benefits

In selling, remember this: People don't buy products. They buy the satisfactions and benefits that will be attained *from* products. No matter what you sell, don't just talk about *features*. Features are facts about the product, service, system, and so forth. Their focus is on the product. Talk *benefits*. Benefits are what those features *mean* to the customer. They focus on the *customer*. Every time you mention a feature, be sure to translate that feature to a corresponding *customer benefit*.

Automatic door locks on a car are a feature. Ease in passenger entry and child safety are benefits.

Carbon steel gears are a feature. Less down-time is a benefit.

An overdrive transmission is a feature. Longer engine life and better gas mileage are benefits.

Let's say you wanted to sell me a lawn mower. It has the following features: Extra-wide 38-inch cut; heavy-duty 12-horsepower engine; it's self-propelled with a seven-speed transmission which will run anywhere between two and five miles an hour; magnesium housing shaped so that it will cut within an inch of fence posts and trees; and a special blade that always cuts level without showing ridges from the wheels. What are the benefits for me?

Got 'em? Wait! Not so fast! I said sell *me* a lawn mower. Are benefits the same for everyone? Are my benefits the same as for, say, my next door neighbors, Fred and Martha?

Let me tell you about Fred and Martha. Fred's retired from the military. I don't know how they stand it, but every morning, 15 minutes before sunrise, Fred and Martha are out working in their yard. A lot of mornings I wave hello to them as I'm getting home. I must say they do have a beautiful yard. It's the pride of the neighborhood. My yard? I can't stand yard work. Just hate it. In the summer I look out at it and say, "Well, Kimball, you've got two choices: You can mow it this weekend, or you can Bush Hog it next weekend."

The benefits? Totally different! For Fred and Martha: a beautiful manicured lawn. And this mower will do all the trimming around the trees and fence posts so they'll have more time to do the things they love to do in the garden. For me: this son of a gun will plow through foot-tall growth at five miles an hour. It'll do the whole lawn in half the time. I can wake up at noon and still get the lawn done in time to watch the Cubbies!

So how do you know which benefits to present to a customer? Hey, you're catching on! You first get them to talk and tell you what's important to them. Listen! What's their hot button? Then translate *your* features into *their* benefits. Sound simple? It really is.

# Secret 5:
# Take a Walk in Your Customer's Shoes

The professional salesperson knows that before you can sell anything to anyone you must first put yourself in the customer's position. Take a walk in your customer's shoes and ask yourself: "All right, if these roles were reversed, if I were the customer and this sales presentation were being made to me, how would I react to it? What kind of things would be important to me and my business? What types of benefits would be important to me and make me want to buy? And why would I want to listen to this salesperson?" By putting yourself in the customers shoes, you take the focus off yourself and *your* needs and put the focus where it belongs, on the customer and *his or her* needs. Let's face it: People buy for *their* reasons, not yours.

Make your customers feel important. Put the spotlight on them. The customer is the star of the show. Talk about their needs, their problems, their opportunities, and what you can do to address them. Look for a mutual benefit. A win-win situation. The customer gets something he or she wants and cares about—benefits—and you get something you want and care about—you get paid. You also get the satisfaction of knowing that you helped that customer attain something important.

Professional salespeople love problems. Not their own, of course. The customer's! Think about it. When you've got a problem, what's on your mind, all the time? Of course! The problem! It just won't go away. And when you've got a problem, what's one of your top priorities? Right again! Getting rid of that problem! OK, so how about putting yourself back in the customer's shoes for a moment. What kinds of problems does your customer have? And what can your products and services do to help? Again, study the features, but find the *benefits* for each customer.

# Secret 6:
# Price Is No Object

Price is no object? What, you say, of course it is! Well, yes, it's true that price is a point to be discussed in the sales presentation. But it's also true that the amateur salesperson concentrates too heavily on price to generate a buying motive. It's an easy trap to fall into. Let me illustrate what I mean.

The following conversation recently occurred at Metro Outdoor Furnishings, a leading retailer of high-quality poolside and patio furniture. The company sells only one line of patio furniture, built with genuine steel tubing and painted with chip-resistant enamel. Its strapping is made to last for 15 years without breaking or losing its shape. Its regular prices are at least 10 percent below those charged at competitive outlets for comparable merchandise. At the time of this conversation, however, Metro's chairs had been reduced from $100 to a sale price of $80, and chaise lounges, normally $190, were on sale for $150. A nicely dressed woman in her 30s drove up to the outlet in a V-12 Jaguar and was looking at samples displayed outside. A salesperson approached her.

Salesman:   "Looking for some patio furniture today?"

Prospect:   "Well, I'm kind of shopping around to see what's available."

Salesman:   "Perfect timing. Normally, our prices are about 10 percent lower than anywhere else in town for comparable merchandise. But this week only, the chairs are specially priced at $80 and the chaises are on sale for $150."

Prospect:   "For all of them?"

Salesman:   "No, ma'am, each."

Prospect:   "$80 for *one* chair? $150 for *one* chaise lounge? That's outrageous!"

Salesman:   "But, ma'am, you won't find these chairs anywhere else for less than $109.95. And the chaises would be at least $209.95."

Prospect:   "Nonsense. I was just at K mart. They had chairs for $6.99 and chaises for $9.99."

Salesman:   "Yes, but let me show you something. These are made with genuine steel tubing instead of lightweight aluminum. Won't chip, won't rust. And look at these straps. Won't break, won't stretch out of shape. Should last 15 years. Wouldn't you agree that these are of higher quality?"

|                |                                                                                                                                                                                                                                                                                                                                                                                                                           |
| -------------- | ------------------------------------------------------------------------------------------------------------------------------------------------------------------------------------------------------------------------------------------------------------------------------------------------------------------------------------------------------------------------------------------------------------------------- |
| Prospect:      | "Of course they're of higher quality. But not enough higher to pay $80 instead of $6.99 or $150 instead of $9.99."                                                                                                                                                                                                                                                                                                         |
| Salesman:      | "Think of it this way. These will last 15 years. Cheap furniture you'll have to replace every year. By the time you put out $6.99 or $9.99 every year for 15 years, you'll have paid as much or more."                                                                                                                                                                                                                       |
| Prospect:      | "That's absolutely ridiculous! Maybe you can get someone else to believe that, but not me. I'm an investment banker and I believe I know a thing or two about money. With your furniture I have to make an outlay of funds every 15 years. With the cheap furniture, I can keep all my money in a money market account earning eight percent a year. On the interest alone, I can buy new furniture every year and never spend my principal." |
| Salesman:      | "But these are much higher quality. You can jump up and down on these and they won't break. What would happen if you did that to cheap furniture?"                                                                                                                                                                                                                                                                          |
| Prospect:      | "Let me assure you that neither I nor any of the guests I invite to my home are the sorts of persons to jump up and down on the patio furniture."                                                                                                                                                                                                                                                                           |
| Salesman:      | "They do look nice, though, don't they?"                                                                                                                                                                                                                                                                                                                                                                                   |
| Prospect:      | "They do at that. But not 15 times as nice."                                                                                                                                                                                                                                                                                                                                                                               |
| Salesman:      | "We have free delivery, too."                                                                                                                                                                                                                                                                                                                                                                                              |
| Prospect:      | "Hmmm. Well, if I change my mind, I'll be back."                                                                                                                                                                                                                                                                                                                                                                           |
| Salesman:      | "Fine. Our sale goes through Sunday. Have a nice day."                                                                                                                                                                                                                                                                                                                                                                     |

So much for that. Sound like a typical day on the job? Could you empathize with the frustrated salesperson? Let's take a look at this sales presentation. How would you rate it? Excellent, good, average, fair, or poor? Of course, this was a pretty tough customer. On the other hand, I haven't seen too many easy customers lately.

Let's go back and look at some of the things we've already talked about in this chapter. Put yourself in the customer's shoes. Find out what she cares about, her hot button, a buying motive. Get her to talk. Ask questions. Listen. Then translate *your* features to *her* benefits. Focus on the customer. How about this patio furniture salesperson? The focus was pretty much on features and price, wasn't it?

In this selling situation, the salesperson didn't make much use of questions that get the customer involved. Nevertheless, the customer volunteered information which could have, and should have, been pursued further. She does what for a living? Investment banking. And she drives a Jag, no less. She's probably doing pretty well for herself, or at least has access to considerable lines of credit. It's highly likely she's a qualified prospect. And the usage of the product? Her guests are not the types to be jumping up and down on the furniture. Apparently, she's not planning any six-keg pig roasts with the local collegiate rugby team. Who is she entertaining? Probably fellow bankers, brokers, and dealmakers, along with an occasional client or two. What kind of home do you think she has? I'll give you odds it's not a 3-bedroom/1½-bath ranch on a quarter-acre lot. Do you begin to see some potential benefits? Sure! She'll be entertaining. It's important to her to convey an image of taste and success. Benefits! Increase the perceived value and bring it closer to price.

Why? Because price is no object! The amateur salesperson focuses on price. Justify the material costs and get the price low enough, and you get the sale, right? Well, sometimes. But more often than not, no. For one thing, how much latitude do you have in your pricing? Probably not that much. And what flexibility you *do* have is likely to be reflected in the profitability of your company and your earnings. Don't get hung up on price. Build *value*. When value received exceeds price paid, you get the sale. You've got two ways to go: Focus on features and price, or key in on benefits and value. The professional salesperson focuses on benefits and value. And the way to do that is to ask questions which involve the customer and let them discover these benefits for themselves.

When people get greater value and more benefits, they gladly pay more. Don't lower the price. Help the customer discover benefits and build value.

# Secret 7:
# Don't Sell Anyone

Amateur salespeople think they need to sell something to someone. Wrong! How about you? What reaction do you have when someone's trying to sell you something? Exactly!

"Excuse me, but I just remembered I forgot to turn off the water when I got out of the shower this morning. Gotta go. See ya later!"

Professional salespeople don't sell anyone. People hate to be sold. But on the other hand, we all *love* to buy. The professional salesperson *helps* us to buy. The problem is, no two people are alike. What hits one person's hot button and motivates him or her to buy may be totally ineffective with the next person. We're all different and buy for different reasons and in a different manner.

Wouldn't it be great if we could come up with something we could quickly and easily use which would help us better understand our prospects and how and why they buy? Well, maybe we can. Let's think about it. For descriptive variables to be useful, they've got to satisfy two criteria:

(1)  They must be readily observable; and

(2)  They must yield reliable predictions of behavior.

In human interactions, there are many such variables, but two particular behavioral dimensions stand out as especially useful.

The first of these is *assertiveness*, which may be defined as the degree of influence a person exerts to control situations and the thoughts, feelings, and actions of others. Readily observable? Sure. Within about a minute of meeting anyone, we can pretty well tell whether that person is highly assertive, not at all assertive, or at some other position on the scale between the two extremes. Nonverbal cues are particularly helpful in determining someone's relative level of assertiveness. Highly assertive people are very active in nonverbal communication. They employ many gestures, make steady eye contact, and tend to speak quickly and at high volume. They generally give you a firm handshake and communicate readily with emphatic statements. When highly assertive people ask questions, it is often to confront or challenge another person and emphasize points of their own. By contrast, people low in assertiveness convey a significantly lower level of nonverbal cues. They employ limited gestures, make only intermittent eye contact and speak slowly, at relatively low volume. Their handshakes are often soft and they tend to communicate hesitantly, with tentative statements. When people low in assertiveness ask questions, it is more likely for the purpose of clarification or to support information. Other characteristics: Highly assertive people usually won't hesitate to let you know how they feel. They'll readily express their opinions. They tend to be fast-paced, impatient, make quick decisions, and are willing to take risks. Just the opposite for those low on the assertiveness scale, who are more likely to be slow-paced, easygoing, and tend to reserve their opinions. They're averse to risk, and, so, often take a lot longer than assertive types to come to decisions.

The second behavioral dimension is *sensitivity*, which may be defined as the degree to which a person outwardly expresses feelings or emotions and develops relationships. This characteristic is readily observable, too, isn't it? Just as with assertiveness, it doesn't take very long to determine whether someone is highly sensitive, not at all sensitive, or somewhere in between. Like the highly assertive person, people who are high in sensitivity are more active in nonverbal cues, especially with gestures and animated facial expressions. People with high sensitivity like to be physically closer to others and touch more often. Their primary focus is relationships and they seek sharing personal feelings with others. Just the opposite for people low on sensitivity. They tend to be facially expressionless, with low levels of nonverbal communication. Individuals low in sensitivity don't like as much touching, and will often place a physical barrier between themselves and others. Their primary focus is tasks and they have little or no interest in sharing personal feelings. Other characteristics: Highly sensitive people are more opinion-oriented, with little emphasis on facts and details. Their conversations center around stories and anecdotes. They're open, dramatic, have a flexible perspective about time, and think in terms of the spirit—rather than the letter—of the law. Those low in sensitivity? They don't want opinions, they want details and documentation. Their conversations focus on facts, tasks, and specific issues. These people are more guarded and controlled, are disciplined concerning time, and think in terms of the absolute letter of the law.

Here's what this is all about. By combining the dimensions of assertiveness and sensitivity, we come up with a predictor of *how people like to buy*. Let's look at four typical *buying styles*.

# (1) The Amiable
# (low assertiveness/high sensitivity)

Famous amiables in history include Marge Simpson, Mamie Eisenhower, and Goofy. There's no mistaking it when you walk into their offices. They'll have personal mementos and pictures of the family and the dog on the desk, with drawings by their child or grandchild on the wall.

There's probably a plant or two to keep them company when no one else is around to talk to. Everything is bright and friendly, with open and informal seating arrangements. Amiables won't want to speak to you from behind a desk, so they'll either set the desk sideways to be able to turn and face you without a barrier in the way, or they'll take a chair and join you face-to-face in the social area of the office. Of course, everyone loves an amiable...when it's your grandmother. No, seriously, don't get the idea that I have anything against amiables. I really don't. It's just that with their combination of low assertiveness and high sensitivity, they're simply delighted to see you. As a salesperson, you'd think I'd welcome such a welcome. I would, except for the fact that the amiable wants to have someone to socialize with for a while, not to do business. Socializing is all well and good, but it won't cover the check to the mortgage company on the first of the month. The amiable is warm, friendly, and supportive, and interested in sharing personal feelings. That's high sensitivity and that's nice. But low assertiveness causes amiables to be weak in setting goals and directing themselves, with a risk-averse nature which makes them slow to make decisions and take actions.

If you sell to top management in large companies, you won't run into many amiables. If you deal with the public at large, you'll come across a lot of them. And they buy things. Therefore, you have to *help* them buy the way they like to buy. Face it: It'll take you a little longer to sell to them because you're going to have to invest time socializing and establishing rapport. Fine. Be agreeable, show a personal interest, and be supportive of their feelings; but keep your selling on track and casually move along slowly and informally.

There are a few things to be careful of in selling to amiables. Remember, amiables don't like to have disagreements or interpersonal conflicts, so they may just go along agreeing with you and telling you what you want to hear. Be sure to get them to spell out their objectives and make it a point to specify exactly what you've agreed to do and when. Forget your computer sheets and marketing research data. They're not into facts and logic. Stay with opinions and personal feelings.

And remember that they don't like risk. Emphasize guarantees and your personal assurances of support. If you sell extended warranties, amiables are a good target: "You'll have no worries for five years, and if you do need service, it'll be great to see you."

# (2)The Expressive
# (high assertiveness/high sensitivity)

Among the best-known expressives of the 20th century are Winston Churchill, Lee Iacocca, and Bill Clinton. In fact, most famous people we like are expressives. It's no secret why. To become famous, it helps to be highly assertive, and to be liked usually requires high sensitivity. Sales managers often prefer to hire expressives as sales reps since they best fit the stereotypical view of the ideal sales personality.

In an expressive's office, you'll probably see "Million Dollar Round-table" or similar awards on the wall, along with slogans such as "When the going gets tough, the tough get going" and autographed pictures from Bear Bryant and Ronald Reagan. The desk will be a mess, cluttered with piles of papers representing the ten or twelve most important projects that person is working on simultaneously. Otherwise, the office decorations and seating arrangements are similar to those of amiables, indicating openness, warmth, and contact.

Because of their high sensitivity, expressives are primarily interested in people and relationships rather than logic, facts, and tasks. They like involvement with others and tend to have gregarious, stimulating personalities, and strive for the fulfillment of higher-level needs such as recognition and self-esteem. Expressives are dreamers and get caught up in their dreams. They love to share with others their vision of what they can be and how they'll make it happen.

It's generally not difficult to get an expressive to talk. The problem arises in trying to guide them to address the agenda and issues which are the purpose of your sales call. Let them talk. Get them talking about their ideas, opinions, and dreams. Then focus your selling effort on developing exciting concepts together that will help to support their dreams. Be sure to include success stories and comments from people they can relate to and whose achievements they admire and would like to emulate. Match their fast pace and be dramatic, enthusiastic, and entertaining: "These ideas are great, and I can help them become a reality for you."

A few caveats in dealing with expressives: Because of their propensity to dream and deal in feelings and opinions, they tend to generalize and exaggerate. That means that you have to be careful to button down all the specific details on precisely what you've agreed to and how and when things will be done. After a meeting with an expressive, be sure to send a follow-up letter saying how great it was talking and adding "As we agreed…", specifying exactly what the next steps will be and the timetables for each. There's nothing wrong with dreaming. Just make sure there's also a firm foundation of reality.

# (3)The Analytic (low assertiveness/low sensitivity)

There are no famous analytics. Oh, maybe Jimmy Carter, though he's more of a mix between amiable and analytic. And maybe that guy who does your income tax, what's-his-name, Henry Block. But even he is more of an expressive—he just has a bunch of analytics working for him.

Have you ever noticed how many analytics wind up marrying an amiable? Guess it makes sense. The amiable can go on babbling for hours at a time about all sorts of trivia, while the analytic is able to tune it all out and continue reading *Forbes* or watching the "Nightly Business Report" on CNN, giving an occasional nod or grunt to indicate interest. (A nod or grunt is usually sufficient feedback and encouragement for an amiable.) As a rule, analytics are not exactly what one would call the life of a party, but give them three or four shooters and almost anything can happen, particularly if they're a closet expressive.

You know you're dealing with an analytic the moment you walk into his or her office. It's a totally organized and functional working environment. Likely there'll be graphs, tables, and charts on the wall, all relating to the company and their job. No pretty pictures unless they serve some specific purpose. The desk top is totally different from that of the expressive, which makes sense since analytics are 180 degrees opposite from expressives. On the desk, there'll probably be an appointment calendar and materials relating to the project at hand. Nothing else. All other items are filed away in their proper place, to be retrieved at the appropriate time. Seating arrangements will be formal and proper, with the desk positioned between you and the analytic to dispel even a hint of contact or intimacy.

Since they're low on both assertiveness and sensitivity, analytics are not what you'd call the most dynamic, warm, and open people. But they do have their hot buttons: Precision, facts, data, and organization. For starters, if you're calling on an analytic, it would behoove you to be on time. To them, 9:02 is *not* 9 O'Clock. Time-disciplined, letter of the law. Also, you would be well advised to double-check and triple-check all your materials for typos or even the most seemingly insignificant omission or error. A few of those probably wouldn't faze an amiable or an expressive. Just one might blow you out of the water with an analytic. With these people, bring along a lot of facts, brochures, supporting data, and computer printouts. Be prepared for questions about specifics, and keep things organized and structured.

The biggest problem with analytics is that they'll analyze things to death. They love analysis so much that making a decision is a letdown. Their fun is over. You're not going to force them into making an immediate decision, so don't try. Give them the facts and tangible supporting evidence. Forget anybody else's opinions, since they have confidence only in their own. But *do* try to structure their options into two or three specific alternatives and try to move them in the direction of deciding *which* alternative best fits their needs, rather than have them plod along aimlessly analyzing interminably. For each alternative, provide them a summation of benefits/advantages vis-à-vis negatives/disadvantages. And remember: Analytics are not risk-takers and want to be sure they're right, so be sure to include guarantees to minimize their risk.

# (4)The Driver
# (high assertiveness/low sensitivity)

Among the better-known drivers are General George Patton, J. Edgar Hoover, and Genghis Khan. If you've ever had the pleasure of dealing with retired military personnel, you can probably recount a few war stories of your own about dealing with drivers. In their offices, these people aren't merely closed and non-contact-oriented, they want to dominate you. They'll sit behind massive desks in chairs elevated so they can look down on you. You'll be in a cushy chair which positions you submissively down and backward toward a corner. On the wall will be plaques from the NRA and the John Birch Society, along with assorted flags, and bayonets from his or her tour of duty in the Persian Gulf. These people don't mess around. They couldn't care less about your feelings or problems or about anyone who cares about anyone's feelings or problems. On the other hand, drivers usually get results. High levels of results. Fast-paced, competitive, decisive, driven for the achievement of goals. They can make things happen. Drivers will do their utmost to dominate you, but if they succeed, they lose respect for you and your cause is lost. Like a pit bull, if they sense fear they go for the throat.

Drivers are highly disciplined, and you need to be, too. As with the analytic, be on time and have all your facts and details buttoned down. Drivers don't want to hear about feelings and are impressed with no one's opinions.

It's important in selling generally, but particularly with drivers, to let them discover the truth for themselves and believe the buying decision was their own idea. Actually, drivers can be fairly easy to control just by letting them think *they're* in control. You do that by identifying and supporting their goals and objectives through the judicious use of questions which lead them to a desired conclusion. Then, help them generate alternative action plans with attendant factual pros and cons of each so they can tell you *how*, not *if*, they're going to buy.

In dealing with drivers, especially if you're an expressive, you may be tempted to try to be personable and get to know them a little better, perhaps become friends. Forget it, unless they convey such an interest themselves. Acknowledge their achievements and ideas, but don't try to relate to them on a personal level. Stick with the facts. Stick with the business at hand.

# Summing Up

What we've seen so far is that this is a book about salesmanship—*professional* salesmanship. We've covered the Seven Top Secrets which make the difference between being "just a salesperson" and an *effective* and *professional* salesperson. To review:

- **Secret 1:** Selling is a learned skill, not an inherent gift. Work hard, develop the skill, and you can be one of the best.

- **Secret 2:** Knowledge. You have to know everything there is to know about your product, customer, competition, and industry. No skimping. No short cuts. You have to be an expert.

- **Secret 3:** The magic word, *listen.* Ask questions. Get your customers to talk. Have them tell you what's important to them, what they care about. Determine their needs, their hot buttons, and their buying motives *before* you start presenting.

- **Secret 4:** People don't buy products, they buy *benefits.* Take the focus off yourself, the product, and its features. Put the focus on the customer and need-satisfying benefits instead.

- **Secret 5:** Take a walk in the customer's shoes. See things from his or her point of view, and translate *your* features to *their* benefits.

- **Secret 6:** Price is no object. The amateur focuses on price and tries to get it low enough to motivate the customer to buy. But the professional builds up *value*. When you build value and benefits to a level higher than the price, you get the sale.

- **Secret 7:** Don't sell anyone, because people hate to be sold. On the other hand, people love to buy. Assess your customer's buying style according to their assertiveness and sensitivity, and get the sale by helping them to buy the way they like to buy.

# You Are the Most Important Product of All

---

## The Six Top Secrets of Knowing Yourself

The most important product of all is, of course, *you*. How many times have you heard people say, "You have to sell yourself"? If you're like me, probably enough times so that you're sick and tired of hearing it. Only one thing, though, it really is true. As we saw in the last chapter, you are a salesperson, and often the product is you, personally, the self-product.

In the marketplace of legal commerce, there are few products without substitutes or alternative sources of supply. If a customer isn't sold on you, the salesperson, chances are he or she will choose to buy from someone else.

Having customers like and trust you is part of the equation. But even more important is that customers recognize your competence and respect your professionalism. You achieve that through personal development and an effective, organized, personal management style. In this chapter, you'll discover the Six Top Secrets of knowing yourself, those elements that build a self-product you'll be proud to represent.

The first secret is that you must accept personal responsibility and accountability for yourself and your life. Then discover who you are, what you stand for, and what it takes to reach your full potential. Part of the formula for success is a winning attitude and a commitment to ethical standards and, also, knowing and confronting your enemy: the time robbers that can steal your productivity. Let's take a look at the Six Top Secrets of Knowing Yourself.

# Secret 1:
# Accept Personal Responsibility and Accountability

I'm sorry to be the bearer of bad news, but the fact is that no one else is going to watch over you. No one is going to take care of you. No one is going to protect you from the rest of the world. And no one is going to help you reach your potential and achieve happiness and success. No one except you, yourself. The base point for building your self-product, then, is to start accepting personal responsibility for yourself, your actions, and the circumstances you're in. Take a good look at yourself and your current situation. Job. Home. Lifestyle. Relationships. Financial situation. Health. Security. Happiness or lack thereof. Everything! If you're like most people, your assessment of life factors will probably yield many items you're very satisfied about and many others you're not. A few factors make you ecstatic, a few others downright depressed. Let's first take those items you're pleased about. How did they get to be that way? Did they just happen to fall on you as random events, or did you in any way influence them? Unless you just hit the lottery, it's likely that you'll identify specific actions you took which caused these things to happen. Actions which, had you not taken them, would not have you enjoying their consequences today. That's all well and good and the way it should be.

Now let's assess those things you're not quite so pleased about and ask how they got to be that way. Again, random events or the result of your actions? "Just a moment," you protest. "Sure, in many ways I'm responsible for this fine mess I've gotten myself into. But there are other people who had a hand in it, too." Oh, really? Who? "Well, my ex-wife/ex-husband, that psychotic tyrant who's my boss, the county zoning board, my neighbor, etc., etc., etc." Stop it, friend, you and you alone are responsible! If someone else did something unpleasant on your behalf, it's because you put yourself in the situation where they could do so.

"Put myself in the situation?" you ask. "Maybe recently, but you can't imagine what it was like for me growing up. My parents! The community! The terrible environment I was exposed to! My traumatic childhood!" Isn't it amazing how many ostensibly mature adults are still citing their parents and childhood as the basis for their current shortcomings? What baloney! Deal with it! Put it behind you. If you're still carrying that sort of excess baggage to rationalize your failures, it's time to drop it and grow up into adulthood. Sure, unfortunate things happened to you. Unfortunate things happen to everyone. But if you're sufficiently enlightened to recognize how such events influenced you, you have the capacity to undo their effects by accepting full responsibility for yourself and your situation from this point forward.

"OK, OK," you say, "I see your point. But I've had some bad breaks." Bad breaks? Of course you have. Probably had some good breaks, too, though, haven't you? How many times have you "lucked out" when a potential disaster loomed ahead? More times than you'd care to think? Hey! Breaks—good or bad—are part of the game. You win some, you lose some. If you seem to be getting more than your share of the bad, almost certainly it's because you weren't doing the right things or doing things right at a critical moment. Down on your luck? You know what luck is, don't you? Luck is the thing that happens when preparation meets opportunity. If you haven't been lucky or had a lot of good breaks lately, better check your preparation.

Something that's been receiving a great deal of attention lately is the plight of what I call the "able-bodied unemployed." Now, certainly, I am sympathetic toward children, old people, and those physically or mentally disabled persons who are unable to earn a living and care for themselves. I believe our society has an obligation to help these people. Similarly, I am sympathetic toward persons who are temporarily out of work, as long as they want to work and are willing to invest the time and energy in getting an education or learning marketable skills. A helping hand, but not a handout.

On the other hand, those persons I refer to as the able-bodied unemployed are in their current situations through no one's fault but their own. They've had chances to work and be productive, but instead have elected to take an alternative course of action and are now reaping the consequences of their decisions. You reap what you sow. Perhaps you may think I'm coldhearted, but I don't feel particularly sympathetic for the able-bodied unemployed.

I am absolutely convinced that each and every one of us has the capacity for achievement. However, I also believe that if someone chooses not to achieve, he or she has the right to fail and wind up in the gutter. Wherever you are, at the pinnacle of happiness and success, or living in a cardboard box and sleeping on a grate, begin now by acknowledging that you and you alone put you where you are. No excuses. No blaming others.

The last few paragraphs may not have been fun reading. If that's the case, so be it. The first necessary step in the self-product is accepting personal responsibility and accountability. Things that happened in the past were the result of what you did or elected not to do. The same holds true for what will happen in the future. Also, forever purge your mind of even the slightest thought that anybody owes you anything. No one owes you a damn thing, particularly a living and happiness. I especially hope that you harbor no illusions about the government taking care of you. If you believe that, just remember my words when you spend your golden years in a tenement slum, with an inoperative heating system, surviving on peanut butter sandwiches.

It's simple: Things will happen for you if and only if you make them happen. Take charge. Understand that the only thing that counts is this day forward. The past is gone and there's nothing you can do about it. Burn the past and put it behind you, but learn from it. Assess the reasons for your successes. Identify how you contributed to your failures, and just don't make the same mistake twice. Move toward the future by living in the eternal now.

# Secret 2:
# Know the Real You

The self-product is you. Your values. Your attitudes. Your personality. All those many characteristics that add up to you. So let me ask you a question: Just who are you, anyhow? No, I don't mean your name. I mean those things which describe *you*. No, not your sex, age, height, weight, social security number, family members, and the lines on your resume. I mean that energy field that contains your identity, feelings, and consciousness. Your attitudes, your feelings, those things that make you feel good, those things that hurt you. Answer honestly: How many people *really* know the  *real* you? And more importantly, do *you* know the real you?

I guess it's safe to say that most of us want to be liked and accepted by others. That's normal and natural. Problem is, there's a flip side to that equation. Because in order to have others like and accept us, we naturally seek to convey those things that will gain us acceptance, and refrain from conveying anything that might result in disapproval or rejection. Nothing wrong with that unless you carry it to an extreme. Then, instead of being your own person, you can fall into conformity for the sake of belongingness. Your inner self and identity is lost. You become shaped by others. A mirror of the organization. A clone of your peer group. A surrender to the consensus.

To have pride in yourself, you have to *like* yourself. To like yourself, you have to *be* yourself, not who and what others think you should be. It may not be easy to do, but take a good look at yourself and ask, "Just who am I, anyhow?" Your beliefs. Your attitudes. Are they really yours or just someone else's that you took on because they seemed right and proper. Your career path and lifestyle choices. Social habits. What you read, watch, and see. Where and how you live. Are they really you or just reflections of what parents and peers determined for you?

What it all comes down to is that the *real* you is *you*. Think back to when I asked how many people really know the real you. Could you think of anyone? If so, I suspect you have an immensely satisfying relationship with that person who accepts the real you.

Be yourself! Search deep inside yourself for the real you, and have pride in being that person. Get along with others, sure, but decide for yourself what's right and what's wrong. What's important or not. What you'll do or won't do. Choose the times and places to take your stand against the tyranny of the majority.

When all is said and done, you've got two ways to go. The first way is to try to be, think, and act as others demand, and hope people will like and accept you for someone you aren't. The alternative is to just be who you really are, have your own personal beliefs and values, and stick to them. This means that you may not always be popular, but if you're concerned about popularity, I'd suggest you go back to high school. Discover and be yourself, and command the *respect* of others. It's the cornerstone of the self-product.

# Secret 3:
# Be All You Can Be

According to an ancient proverb, a journey of a thousand miles begins with a single step. That first single step is discovering and being yourself. Achievement of your full potential is the journey, and it's the focus of the remainder of this chapter.

Generally, I'm not too hot on motivational slogans, but I do like the one in the Army promotionals: "Be all you can be." That says it all. You only come this way once. I just can't imagine anything worse than waking up in latter middleage and realizing that you really hadn't done much of anything significant, and that now it was too late to get on with it. "What might have been" are truly the saddest words of tongue or pen. I might have done this. I should have done that. No way!

Think of it like this. The first 18 years of your life just get you through childhood. Anything past age 65 is bonus time. What that means is that you've got about 47 years, or just over 17,000 days, for everything. Not a lot of time. Chances are you're already over 18. Take the number of years till 65 and multiply by 365. Not a lot of time at all. Better get off your backside starting today.

The first step toward becoming all you can be is being, liking, and respecting yourself. Pride. Believing you're a decent person. Not perfect by any means. We all occasionally fall off the path and into the mud, but it's those times which help us differentiate between a pig and an achievement-oriented person. A pig falls in the mud and remains there wallowing in it. An achievement-oriented person—a winner—gets up, cleans off, and gets back on the path to continue the journey, having learned from the mistake and being careful not to repeat it.

Another attribute necessary to become all you can be is self-discipline, the resolve to do what has to be done. Sacrifice. Not out of fear of punishment from someone else, but a willingness to do those things necessary and consistent with the commitment to excellence in everything you do. Part of that is doing what you say you'll do. I'm sure this has happened to you: Someone tells you they'll call Wednesday or Thursday to make plans for the weekend. They don't. You see them Monday and they say, "Gee, I got busy. Guess I forgot to call." Or someone borrows an item which you absolutely, positively must have back in three days. They assure you it will be returned on time. Four days later, guess what? A salesperson promises you something will be given personal attention. It falls through the cracks. The list goes on. You get irritated when people tell you they'll do things and they don't. Justifiably! Resolve now, then, not to be guilty of such indiscretions yourself. If you say you're going to do something, do it. If you're not sure you're going to do it, don't say you will. Perhaps say "I may do it," or "Right now, I think I'll do it, and if I do decide to, I'll let you know by Friday." That way, you haven't committed yourself to anything. But when you say you *will* do something:

- Write it down.

- Do what you said you'd do when you said you'd do it.

Business or personal. No difference. If, on a *rare* occasion when something unexpected comes up, get back in touch with that person *immediately* and say something to the effect, "I told you yesterday that I'd do such-and-such by Wednesday, and now I find it'll be Friday." Take your lumps. You said you'd do something and now you won't. They may not be happy. Fine. They have just cause. But whatever happens, they'll respect you more than if you'd just let it ride. Get up out of the mud and get back on the path, learning that the next time it might be better to say, "I expect to do such-and-such by Wednesday, but if it'll be any later than that, I'll get back to you."

Some of these examples may seem like little details, but that's part of effective self-discipline: Attention to lots of little details which aggregate to an impression of competence.

"All you can be" may be a lot more than you think it can be. All of us are capable of achieving just about anything if we make the commitment to excellence, focus on a goal, and are willing to pay the price.

I'd like to share with you a personal experience along those lines that really hit me in the face. A few years ago, a friend and I had just finished running a few miles at a local track and were walking a few laps to cool down. He asked me if I thought I'd ever run a marathon. My response was that I didn't think I was capable of it, that I was rapidly approaching 40, and had never run more than 12 miles in my life. A few months later I saw a news clip about the person who had just finished last in the New York City Marathon. Crippled, she required an aluminum walker, and it took her from 8:00 A.M. until 1:00 A.M. the next morning to do the 26 miles, but she did it. She ran a marathon. I can vividly remember taking stock at that moment and saying, "Well, Kimball, you can stop fooling yourself here and now. If you don't ever do a marathon, it's not because you're not capable of it. It's because you didn't make up your mind to do it, and you weren't willing to pay the price."

Amazing as her accomplishment was, a few years later the person who came in last had no legs. He was on a board, holding blocks in his hands and striking them against the pavement to move himself forward a foot at a time. It took him several days, but that dude ran a marathon.

The bottom line is that all you can be is all you want it to be. You can do anything. Just make it happen.

# Secret 4:
# The Winning Attitude: Think Like an Achiever

If you're going to be an achiever, you've got to start thinking like an achiever. Achievement and success are an attitude. Mediocrity and failure are an attitude. If you're an achiever, you set high standards and have a commitment to personal excellence in everything you do. Without high standards and a commitment to excellence, you're a failure waiting to happen.

Achievement and success are born out of desire and enthusiasm. See the abundance and go for it. Fellow achievers can feel your positive motivating force, and it stimulates them as well. Among achievers, who can help but get excited by someone who is genuinely enthusiastic? Among achievers—winners—enthusiasm is contagious. The problem is, among losers, excuses and lethargy are just as contagious.

We've already hit on excuses. There are none. We accept full responsibility for ourselves and our situation. But from losers, you'll hear a lot of excuses. Some almost sound plausible. Who wants to accept blame for their own misery? Remember the Bob Seger song "Beautiful Loser"? I always found that to be a contradiction in terms, an oxymoron. Losers are losers. That's all there is to it.

We've all known our share of losers, and there's only one thing we can do with them. Let them go. Leave them behind. You may have tried to befriend and help a few losers in your day. If so, I suspect you got burned. You saw people who, to use an analogy, were over their heads and drowning, so you got in a boat and paddled out to help them. But instead of letting you pull them into the boat to safety, all they could do was to try and pull you in the water to drown with them.

The losers of the world can do nothing but drag you down. An enthusiastic, winning attitude is a threat to them. Makes them uncomfortable. You can always depend on the losers to tell you not to try something and why you'll fail if you do. Don't expect encouragement from these people. To remain popular with your loser friends, there's a price: Forget achievement and accept mediocrity. A bit too high a price to pay, isn't it?

There are plenty of winners in the world. Surround yourself with them. Catch each other's enthusiasm. Revel in each other's successes. Identify with and be with the kinds of people you respect and would like to emulate. And those old loser friends, what do you say to them? Say nothing. They're not going to listen. They don't want to hear it. Just get busy doing other things with other people—winning people. If you want to do something to help the less fortunate people of the world, do volunteer work or contribute to service organizations that help children or others whose situation is no fault of their own. Work to enable people to help themselves. But when the losers come calling, don't be home.

When you begin associating with winners, you're going to discover something interesting about their perspective on failure. Winners fail a lot, and they cherish their failures. That might seem strange. We tend to think of failure as something to be avoided, and that a winning attitude would minimize failure. In fact, just the opposite is true. It's the losers who are afraid to fail, and thus won't attempt anything they're not sure they can do. And when losers do fail, the experience is nothing more than negative reinforcement, further convincing them that they've got such tough lives with so many bad breaks. They don't learn from failure or alter their future behavior, and that virtually guarantees repeated failure. Wallowing in the mud.

What a difference with the winners! No, they may not particularly enjoy failure at the time, but they see it as a necessary component of personal growth. If you haven't failed, you haven't tested your potential. Winners try. Winners test themselves. Winners give it their best shot. When they succeed, they relish the fruits of victory. When they fail, they see failure not as an end in itself but as an opportunity for assessment. What did they do right? What did they do wrong? What worked? What didn't? Then they go back out and try again, aiming even higher and with an increased probability of success.

How about yourself? Had any significant failures lately? If not, maybe it's time. You know what's holding you back, don't you? One thing: Fear! Fear of failing! Think about it. I'll bet there's something you'd really like to do, or someone you'd really like to meet, but you're holding back. Why? Fear of failure or fear of rejection, isn't it? But when you look at it, what's the worst thing that could happen? The very worst. What, if anything, is your downside risk, the loss if you fail? Compare that to the upside potential if you succeed. What's your probability of success? It might be time to give it a shot.

On my thermostat at home, there's a range called the "comfort zone." That's fine for the house. Not for your life. Losers seek to be comfortable, to avoid pain and failure. And let's be honest: Failure, particularly on a personal level, can be very painful. But if you're always comfortable, you're not growing.

Winners see comfort as only a brief interlude between periods of growth. They move *toward* the rewards of achievement instead of *away from* the unpleasantness of failure. And sure, they fail a lot. That's how they learn and grow. Take a close look at your failures and cherish the lessons they provide, then stand up and get back on the path.

# Secret 5:
# Doing Right or Wrong
# in Business

Lately, there's been a lot of talk about ethics, or the lack thereof, in business. I find it interesting that people refer to ethics as a dilemma, inferring that we're torn between:

1) Doing what's "ethical" and in the best interest of others; versus

2) Doing what's "unethical" and in our personal best interest.

Implicit in that message is the suggestion that it's not in my personal best interest to be ethical. That, my friends, is an erroneous assumption or, as we say down on the farm, pure hogwash.

Let's look at it this way. Professional selling gives you the power to influence others. You can use that power unethically to manipulate people into acting against their best interest in order to make your sale. But only once. Because when they figure out—which they will—that you used them, I can guarantee you this: They'll never buy anything from you again. And they'll tell three people a *day* to beware of you.

On the other hand, you can use this power ethically to help others achieve benefits they want and need. And when they start enjoying those benefits you've provided them, they will gladly recommend you to others. If you've been in sales for even a few years, you know there's one thing critical to long-term success: referrals from satisfied customers. And using your power ethically generates these referrals.

In selling, it's not a question of being ethical versus making money. If it were, it would present us with a difficult dilemma: Be unethical and rich, or ethical and starve. The fact is, honesty pays. Doing things for customers when and only when it's in their best interest. Having integrity. Giving and taking value-for-value openly and fairly. Do unto others. What goes around comes around. So who needs ethics? We all do. For our own good reasons.

# Secret 6:
# Know Thine Enemy

How about it? Feel pretty good about your self-product? I hope so, because now it's time to get organized and down to business. And to do that, you'll need to know your enemy. No, I don't mean your competition. You already know all about them. I mean your *real* enemy. It looks innocent enough; it's a cute, cuddly, furry little critter. However, that little critter has ten fangs that will get you every time if you're not prepared. That critter is Ineffective Time Management and the ten fangs are the Ten Time Robbers that can tear your best intentions to shreds.

Effective time and territory management isn't a luxury. It's a necessity if you're going to make things happen. If you're like me, there never seems to be enough time to get everything done. And it's true, there *isn't* enough time. The solution, then, is to make *better use* of our existing time. That means knowing the enemy of ineffective time management and watching out for its fangs, the Ten Time Robbers.

# Time Robber 1:
# Failure to Set Goals and Prioritize

Everything else we talk about in this chapter is important, too, but nothing more so than the need to prioritize and set goals. I'm sure you've heard the old saying, "When you're up to your knees in alligators, it's difficult to remember that your primary objective is to drain the swamp." In sales, as in most professions, fire fighting comes with the territory, and it's easy to fall into the trap of believing that fighting fires takes priority over anything else. Perhaps it seems so, but if you're *react-ing* to events as they occur, instead of *proactively* setting priorities and *causing* things to happen, you're in trouble. Time to pull back on the reins, stop, take a deep breath, and reassess. We agree there aren't enough hours in the week to do everything you'd like to do. That's why it's essential to be sure you're doing the right job, not just doing the job right. You're probably familiar with the Pareto Principle, or the 80-20 Rule. Twenty percent of your customers give you 80 percent of your business. Twenty percent of your employees give you 80 percent of your hassles. And specifically, 20 percent of your time, spent on the "vital few" tasks, yields 80 percent of your positive results. By contrast, that other 80 percent of your time, spent on the "trivial many," yields only 20 percent of the positive results.

The objective of prioritizing is to achieve *your* priority goals plus routine tasks by setting priorities which permit flexibility for handling crises, interruptions, and impositions of the boss and "the system." You do that by first identifying the "vital few" and being sure to do them. Then, you determine the "trivial many" and decide what you're not going to do. That's right: *Not do*. Delegate or eliminate! Add a new word to your vocabulary: Just say "No."

I'm big on writing things down. Ideas floating around in your head are great as daydreams, but unlikely to actually happen unless committed to paper.

Stop here and do this. Take a pad of paper and write down *everything* you should, must, or would like to do. Include personal and family goals, everything. If it's a special non-recurring activity, like "Lose 30 pounds," "Quit smoking," or "Walk across Antarctica," include a date for its completion. Without a specific date, it's a daydream and not a goal. Don't expect to complete this in one sitting. Keep the pad out where you can see it frequently and as you think of something, add to the list over a period of a few days.

When you feel the list is complete—when it includes *everything* you can possibly think of doing—you're ready for the fun part. It's time to prioritize.

Every day has 24 hours, and there are seven days in a week, so you have exactly 168 hours for everything you need to do in the next week. From those 168 hours, you must first subtract time required for personal management activities such as sleep, cleaning up, preparing and eating meals, necessary chores, and commuting. Generally, those activities will take about 92 hours per week, leaving 76 hours remaining. Next, subtract time on the job over which you have no control: boss- and system-imposed time, meetings, and other necessary activities. Don't forget to allocate time for the inevitable crises. If you're lucky, you might have 50 hours for all remaining personal, professional, and family activities.

Now go back to your list and estimate how much time you'll need to do everything else. Add it up. It should come as no surprise that the total is considerably higher than the time available. Simply put, some things will get done and some will not. It's up to you to determine what's most important and do those things. Similarly, be sure that what doesn't get done are the least important things.

Your first step is to identify the "vital few." Determine those items that will take up only 20 percent of your remaining time but will account for the highest percentage of positive results. If you wish, select just a portion of an item if you can break it down into component parts. No cheating. You can designate only 20 percent of your remaining time, no more, as activities of highest value and primary concern. These are "A" priorities.

Now go back to your list and select items which will account for another 20 percent of your remaining time, activities of medium value and secondary importance. These are "B" priorities. Designate everything else as a "C" priority, something of low value you can do without.

# Time Robber 2: No Plan

Setting goals and assigning priorities is the first thing you have to do. Having a plan is what puts priorities into action. Perhaps you've heard this truism: Plan your work and work your plan. Many people—until now, you may have been one of them—say they're too busy fighting fires to take time to plan. Roughly translated, what this really means is that if you don't know where you're going, any road will take you there.

Planning requires a little time, of course. But every minute you invest in planning will pay you back five minutes in the time that it takes for execution. Results might be a good bit better, too. No time to plan? Nonsense. Planning is an "A" priority. How about taking a "C" you've been doing and eliminating it. Take that time to plan.

If you've listed and prioritized all your activities, the hard part is already done. Planning just amounts to organizing and scheduling the top priorities. Start with a long-term planning calendar that gives you at least six to twelve months. This gives you the "big picture" of important commitments and activities down the road, and helps you focus on deadlines and sequences of events. For instance, your annual territory plan might be due the first of November. That could mean that all data would have to be ready by the first of October to give you a month to prepare and process the document. That, in turn, could mean that you would need to initiate data collection by the first of September.

The big picture also keeps you aware of blocks of time you need to work around: vacations, sales meetings, the holidays, and the like. Each week, look over the big picture and your master list of prioritized goals

to write your weekly plan. Yes, *write* your weekly plan. Designate a certain time every week to do this. Maybe Friday afternoon, maybe Monday morning, maybe sometime in between, but designate a specific time
and do it then or sooner. Start by writing down all the specific activities
that need to be done in the next week to address each "A." Draw a line
at the end of these activities. Next write down all the specific activities
that need to be done in the coming week for each "B." Another line.
Repeat the same process for each "C." Guess what? You've just generat-
ed your weekly planning guide.

Finally, it's time to break the plan down to the day. If you're not currently using a daily appointment calendar with 15 minutes per line, it's
no wonder you're running around like a chicken with its head cut off.
Jot this down: Get a daily appointment calendar by tomorrow.

When you do your weekly plan, go through your daily appointment
calendar and block out your committed times for the upcoming week.
This should give you a feel for the relative amount of discretionary time
at your disposal on a day-by-day basis, and a sense of what you need to
do on the first day of the week.

Finally, you're ready to do your daily plan. And I mean *daily*. On Sun-
day night, you may be able to block out appointments and other commitments for Friday, but there's no way you can do Friday's accurate
daily plan until Thursday night or Friday morning. Why? Because try as
you might, nothing ever goes exactly as planned.

The key to the daily plan is to keep it current, and that means making up a new one every day. Write down, in order of priority, the most
important things that have to be done that day, and schedule the most
important things first. At the top of the list, designate an "A-1" priority,
the most important item of all. When it's completed, cross it off and
designate a new "A-1." Most important of all, until each "A" has been
completed, don't touch a "B" or "C." Only when the "A's" are done can
you move to a "B," and only when the "B's" are done can you move to
a "C."

Especially when you have just a small block of time at your disposal, it
can be tempting to clean up a small "C" since you can't complete an
"A." But don't yield to the temptation. Even if an "A" can't be completed, do a little piece of it rather than a complete "C." This happened to
me today. I knew I didn't have time to finish this chapter—my "A-1"
this week—and was tempted to knock off early and catch a Star Trek
rerun. I didn't, though.

# Time Robber 3:
# Inefficient Territory Management

I've heard salespeople talk—brag, actually—about driving 50,000 miles on their job last year. Apparently, they believe their odometer measures persistence, determination, and success rather than time wasted sitting behind the wheel. Look at it this way: In a rural territory you might net out 50 miles an hour when you're in your car. That's 1,000 hours a year, or about 20 hours a week, doing nothing but playing Road Warrior. In an urban territory you might net 40 miles an hour, at best. You spend 1,250 hours a year, or about 25 hours a week, behind the wheel.

Yes, cellular phones and in-dash fax machines help, but there's no way you can operate as efficiently in your car as in your office. And neither car nor office is any substitute for meeting prospects and customers in person. Additionally, if you hadn't noticed, cars are not cheap. Including everything, it's got to be costing you at least 40 cents a mile to run it. Think that's high? Just see what they'll offer you on a trade-in for a two-year-old cream puff with 100,000 miles on it. At 40 cents a mile, it's costing you $20,000 to drive 50,000 miles a year. And that's nothing! How much income do you think you're losing by spending as much as half your working hours sitting in traffic?

Keep all this in mind when you do your weekly and daily plans, and make an effort to consolidate calls in a given geographic area. If you need to see a customer in the southeast segment of your territory on Monday, schedule calls on other customers in that segment for that same day. If you need to do a little prospecting, allocate some time to do it when you're in the area on other business rather than making a special trip.

How much time are you killing acting as a delivery person or errand boy, and what is it costing you? No, I don't mean just the 40 cents a mile. Take your annual income and divide it by the number of hours a year you actually spend selling, in person or on the phone. If you're making $50,000 a year with 1,000 hours actually selling, that's $50 an hour! Instead of wasting an hour running a widget out to a customer, call a cab and have them deliver it. Think about it! That doesn't cost, it pays.

# Time Robber 4:
# Crisis Management/Recurring Crises

Something you're going to notice is that many of the other time wasters begin to become less of a problem once you address:

(1) Setting goals and priorities, and

(2) Having a plan

Doing both of these certainly cuts out many potential crises. Remember, some events become crises due to inadequate planning or procrastination. If you're facing a deadline and your schedule hasn't built in flexibility for delays, problems, and the like, you're setting yourself up for a crisis.

And let's face it, there's no way to eliminate *all* the crises that spice up our life. No matter how well you plan, there will be some you just had no way to foresee; so when you write up your weekly and daily plans, be sure to allocate time for the inevitable crises. Remember Murphy's Law: Anything that can go wrong, will, at the least opportune moment. Ask yourself what could go wrong and be prepared with a contingency plan to handle it.

A crisis one time is back luck. The same crisis repeated is bad planning. If you spend more time than you'd like fighting fires, evaluate and classify those crises. Chances are you'll find that certain people, projects, products, etc., are repeatedly at the heart of the problem. Address those issues and take steps in advance and you might avoid a crisis before it happens.

This principle was demonstrated to me early in my business career. I was working in marketing research at the time, and every April we faced the annual crisis of grinding out all the numbers for the brand planning situation review. It was about a month of nights and weekends—no fun. What was strange about it all was that we all just accepted and expected this annual crisis as if it were unavoidable. Sound familiar? Maybe you're so used to your regular crisis cycle that you've become reactive instead of proactive, too. Well, all of a sudden we got a new boss. He was aware of our annual April crisis, but instead of preparing to react to it, he began meeting with the brand planning people in January to determine needs and activities in advance. Son of a gun! Along came April and no crisis.

# Time Robber 5:
# Unnecessary and Unimportant Tasks

Planning and prioritizing should knock a chunk out of this time robber. Remember, too, that even with "A" items you don't necessarily have to do all the work yourself. If you have a staff, or at least some secretarial support, there may be numerous tasks which are candidates for delegation. Instead of composing a routine letter, let your secretary do it. It may not have occurred to you, but secretaries can think as well as type.

Additionally, take a look at some of the arduous busywork you're doing and consider hiring someone to handle it. Do you prospect with direct mail? I trust you routinely send thank-you notes and other information to your current customers. These are definitely "A" items. But that certainly doesn't mean you should be addressing and stuffing envelopes. How about telephoning? You may regularly make cold calls to arrange appointments with prospects. However, why should you be making calls just to gather routine information if someone else could just as easily do so? Go back to your calculations of how much you made for each hour of selling time—you divide annual income by the number of hours actually spent selling. That's the secret. An hour freed up from stuffing envelopes is an hour you can be out selling. Why not consider hiring a high school or college student for ten to twenty hours a week at a fair hourly rate to handle those routine tasks? Again, that doesn't cost, it pays.

# Time Robber 6:
# The Phone

Oh, the phone—the greatest and worst invention in the history of the world. Properly used, the phone can magnify your productivity immensely. Mismanaged, it can bog you down in the quagmire.

I know many businesspeople who answer their own phones. They believe it adds a personal touch. Of course, if you don't have a secretary, you don't have any choice. But if you do, let your secretary or assistant pick up the phone and screen your calls. A well-trained assistant can protect you from people you have no interest in speaking to. Every caller should be asked to state a valid reason for calling and a justification for speaking to you. If a caller does that, let them be put through. Should they fail to do so, there's no point wasting time by taking the call. The two or three minutes it takes to answer an unsolicited call may not sound like much, but multiply that by several dozen events a day and you've got yourself a nice little chunk of time to work on an "A." Additionally, if your calls are screened by an assistant, you'll find the assistant can often handle the matter without bothering you, delegate it, or take a message with the information needed for a callback.

Whether you do or do not have a secretary or assistant, I have several other suggestions for the phone. First, consider establishing designated phone times when you receive and return calls. Just before lunch and late in the day may work out best. When people are ready to go eat or go home, they're more likely to get to the point rather than socialize. The designated phone time also helps you look more professional in the eyes of your customers, since they can depend on times to get through to you or have you get back to them.

Be sure to watch yourself about socializing. Three or four minutes a call rehashing a ball game or a fishing trip can add up fast. Didn't Shakespeare say something about tomorrow and tomorrow and tomorrow makes a pretty good hole in the week? On the phone, four minutes and four minutes and four minutes makes a pretty good hole in the day.

One last thing about the phone. After a call, make any necessary notes right then and there, before you forget. And when possible, take appropriate action immediately or, at the very least, note any required follow-up on your list of priorities.

# Time Robber 7: Paperwork

It is often said that Hitler's army ran on paperwork. Good thing. Otherwise, he might have won the war. I've heard many good salespeople say that the one thing they really hate about their job is the paperwork. Unfortunately, paperwork is here to stay and it's just something you're going to have to deal with. And the fact is, if there's one thing that really bothers a sales manager, it's a salesperson whose paperwork is either consistently late or consistently inadequate. Make your paperwork an "A" and make it manageable for you.

Not all paperwork requires the same level of dedication, however. Some has to be absolutely correct: customer orders, expense accounts, anything for the IRS, and the like. By contrast, there are other things which do not require such a high standard of accuracy. For example, if a staff member wants you to record competitive display activity and count the number of cases featured on an end cap, what difference does it make if there are 190 cases instead of 200 or 210? It's "about" a 200-case display—what's the point of counting every bottle or can?

And why let paperwork pile up all week and be forced to kill half a day Saturday plowing through it, when you've forgotten half the information anyway? I have a solution. Unless you're really big on recurring crises—like traffic tieups and trying to find a parking place in the customer's lot—I trust you always plan to reach an appointment 15 minutes early. Add to that the fact that the customer is always five or ten minutes late inviting you in to their office. Except, of course, when you're running late. How much time a week do you spend in the reception area, along with six other salespeople, blankly gazing at the potted plants or leafing through the six-month-old copies of *Ad Age*? Put that time to work! Update the expense account and call reports. Compose memos. Write plans. Don't just sit there, do something!

Some people think of paperwork as what you write, but that is only half the story. Paperwork also includes all that stuff you're supposed to *read*. And little of that deserves your complete attention. Be selective in what you read. If at first glance you know it's not important, go no further. Trash it then and there. If it does seem to have value, scan the table of contents and just hit the most important sections. Try reading just the first sentence of each paragraph. For articles, restrict yourself to the abstract at the beginning and the "Conclusions" section at the end. And remember to use those minutes waiting before an appointment to catch up on that paperwork you have to read as well as write.

# Time Robber 8:
# Socializing

Socializing with customers—to a point—is part of effective selling. You have to get them relaxed and you want to build rapport before moving to the business at hand. If you're dealing with amiables, you'll do more of it than with analytics or drivers; but in any case, do no more socializing than necessary to break the ice. If you're an amiable or an expressive yourself, you need to be careful not to over-socialize and have customers perceive you're wasting their time with chit-chat.

What really makes socializing a time robber, though, is time spent in the office or the local coffee shop socializing with your fellow salespeople. Those conversations are predictable, anyhow. Everyone just sits around complaining about how lousy business is and about what a jerk the sales manager is. That's because the productive salespeople are out prospecting and meeting customers, generating business. Sales managers love people who produce. People who sit around complaining don't produce.

If you're guilty of spending more than a few quick minutes of socializing with your peers, think about it. Half an hour socializing could instead be spent making ten or twelve cold calls. Chances are that will mean being shot down ten or twelve times. It might also mean one sale that wouldn't have been made otherwise. But you won't know if you don't try. It may also mean you won't be as popular with your peers who want you to sit around and complain. But the truth is, people who sit around complaining instead of doing something, are losers, anyhow. Who needs to be popular with them?

# Time Robber 9:
# Unproductive Meetings

I guess this one should be directed more at sales managers than salespeople. Sales managers call meetings. Salespeople merely have to endure them. If you're a salesperson at the limit of your endurance, you might want to photocopy this section and anonymously slip it on the sales manager's desk.

For starters, meetings should have a purpose. If you have a weekly sales meeting, ask why. Is it just because you always have a weekly sales meeting? Not sufficient! If the same information can be conveyed one-on-one or by memo more effectively, delete it from the meeting agenda. And be sure you always have a meeting agenda. Send it out in advance to all the designated participants and stick to it.

I'm sure you've had this experience. You show up at 8:58 for a 9:00 meeting and about half the designated participants are there. By 9:05, a few more have shuffled in, and someone says, "Go see if so-and-so and what's-her-name are going to be here," and an underling goes out to try to herd them up. At this point, a couple of the early arrivals decide they have just enough time to grab a cup of coffee or make a quick phone call. Around 9:20, the meeting leader mumbles, "Well, I guess we should get started," and rushes through the agenda to make a 10:00 commitment.

That scenario is inexcusable. Meetings start on time. Meetings end on time. If you're in charge of a 9:00 meeting, start it at the exact time. Close and lock the doors so that late arrivals will have to knock to get in and will sheepishly take their seats saying, "Sorry I'm late." I predict you will have to do this exactly once. From that point forward, attendees will be in their seats at 8:59, ready to get started.

Here's another thing I'm sure you've experienced. You're in an hour-long meeting and only five minutes of it applies to you. How frustrating! Participants should attend only those segments which apply to them. It's the duty of the meeting leader to arrange the agenda accordingly or have a separate meeting for each portion and the people who need it. Along the same lines, don't you love it when two people in a meeting engage in a one-on-one dialogue, which concerns no one else, for fifteen minutes while the rest of the attendees sit on their thumbs? Let them hold that conversation alone with each other after the meeting.

Finally, after the meeting, a written summary should be distributed *that day* on what transpired, what was decided, and who is responsible for any follow-up. At the bottom of the summary, calculate the total dollar cost of the meeting—not just the sandwiches and paper clips, either. Add in the people costs. If someone makes $40,000 a year, by the time you add in expenses and benefits, that person probably costs the company $80,000 a year. Figuring 2,000 hours a year, that person costs the company $40 an hour. If you're partially or wholly on commission for a living, that meeting costs *you* $40 an hour. If you have 20 people like that in a meeting which lasts an hour, the people cost is $800. If the results of that meeting fail to put at least $800 on the company's bottom line, its cost is unjustified and the meeting should not have been held.

# Time Robber 10:
# Ineffective Communication

I saved this time robber for last because it's probably the most pervasive of all. More than anything else, ineffective communication is the result of a failure to listen *enough* and to listen *well enough*. And, it's a failure to have clear and explicit meanings in what is communicated. Finally, ineffective communication includes a lack of awareness of how to send and receive messages being broadcast across the many communication channels. This subject is so important it deserves a chapter of its own—Chapter Three, coming up next.

# Summing Up

The purpose of this chapter was to uncover the Six Top Secrets of the most important product of all: you, the self-product. To review:

- **Secret 1:** Finding someone to watch over you. That person is you and you alone. Accept full responsibility and accountability for yourself and your situation. No one else can do it. Success or failure, winning or losing, it's in your hands.

- **Secret 2:** Answer the question, "Just who are you, anyhow?" Discover your true self, your beliefs, your values, and take pride in being the person you are.

- **Secret 3:** Become all you can be. Achieve your full potential by making a commitment to excellence, having high standards, and developing the self-discipline to do what has to be done.

- **Secret 4:** The winning attitude. Break ranks with losers and join the winners. Cherish your failures as lessons for growth.

- **Secret 5:** Know the difference between right and wrong, and conduct yourself ethically in everything you do because it's in your best interest to do so.

- **Secret 6:** Know thine enemy. Your *real* enemy is ineffective time management. Watch out for this little critter's fangs, the Ten Time Robbers.

# Learn the Basics for Effective Communication

## The Six Top Secrets of Communication

It seems as though hardly a day passes without hearing something about the "communications revolution." Satellites, cable, fax, cellular phones, and all the rest. Telecommunications companies assure us, in 30-second bits, about all the great things that are happening. Well, I have two words about the communications revolution: Forget it. There has been no revolution. In fact, there has been no progress whatever in interpersonal communications since the invention of language and, arguably, since the dawn of time. The truth is we're not very good at communicating.

Yes, I readily agree that we have witnessed great progress in information transmission. High-speed computers and innovative modes for sending, receiving, storing, and sharing all the bites and bits the analytics can quantify. The technological advances are impressive. In the past, an employee with a good secretary could grind out 40 or 50 pages of data and text a week. Now, every on-line printer in the marketing research department is spewing out a depth of three feet of computer printouts a day. For many of us, it's gotten to the point where there's so much information that we're having trouble sifting through it all trying to figure out what's important and where it is.

The point is that information transmission is not tantamount to effective communication. And in this era of high technology, we'd better start thinking communication first, transmission second. Otherwise, all the scientific advances will only leave us smothered in data rather than enhance communication.

In this chapter, we're going to take a look at some of the basics of communication. And I do mean basics. For instance, I'm not going to get into public speaking or making formal statements to an audience. There are already plenty of good books which discuss that quite nicely. Also, I won't touch on the sales presentation and demonstration since that's the subject of Chapter Five. This will be communication *basics*, those things you need to consider before you even plan to make a sales call, phone for an appointment, write a letter, or meet anyone face-to-face.

There are Six Top Secrets of Communication. The first is that there is no way we can *not* communicate. No matter where you are, no matter what you're doing, you are continuously sending and receiving messages through the five dimensions of communication. Successful salespeople understand that effective communication consists of both facts and feelings, logic as well as emotion. Management of all those communication cues can help you to convey the intended message and project the desired impression.

# Secret 1: You Are Always Communicating

You can't *not* communicate. Once you turn it on, there's simply no way to shut it off. Think about that for a moment. Sure, when you're face-to-face with someone, actively engaged in conversation, you're communicating. But what if you're just in the background, saying nothing, merely observing? Are you communicating then? Of course! You're receiving messages from others, and as we'll note shortly, communication involves receiving as well as sending. But are you only receiving? Just because you're mute, observing a conversation and sending no verbal messages of your own, does that mean you're not transmitting meaningful concepts through other nonverbal channels? Of course you are. Facial expressions, eye behavior, posture, and gestures may communicate—far more dramatically than words—your reactions to the events at hand. And a lack of nonverbal feedback conveys a message of its own, probably boredom, disinterest, and a desire to be somewhere other than where you are at the moment. Try this: When two people are talking, casually observe the audience. No one else may be speaking, but everyone is communicating messages ranging from apt attention and admiration to controlled contempt and disgust. Wherever you are, among a group of friends or making a presentation to your Board of Directors, can you afford to miss any of these messages? Obviously, you can't. And similarly, even when you're not speaking, shouldn't you be aware of the messages you're conveying to others? Obviously, you should, because you can't *not* communicate. At all times, then, you should consciously determine what it is you wish to be communicating and be sure you're conveying the appropriate messages.

Most of us will probably agree that we can't *not* communicate while in the presence of others. But what if you go home, lock the doors, close the drapes, and unplug the phone? Surely you're not communicating then, are you? Or are you? True, you're not transmitting any specific verbal or nonverbal messages to any specific person at any specific moment, but does that mean you're not communicating and that people aren't receiving meaningful concepts from you? If you consider this for a moment, I believe you'll see that your lack of specific messages may be communicating a great deal and that your silence is deafening.

Let me give you a few examples. I'm sure all of these have happened to you. You're a member of an organization, a committee, or just part of a group of friends who regularly get together, let's say once a week. One week you don't make the meeting, explaining that you were unable to attend due to "a prior commitment" or a "development which required your attention." If you told them this in advance, giving your regrets and assuring them you'd see them all again next week, what have you communicated? Implicitly, you've conveyed the message that there are activities—whatever they may be—which have taken precedence over the group this day.

Let's take it a step further. A week later you attend and remain relatively subdued, not speaking a lot. Two weeks later you again call, giving your regrets. Three weeks later you don't call and you don't show. Have you stopped communicating? Hardly. In fact, your communication three weeks later may be the "loudest" of all: You are drifting away from the group and have elected to do other things, perhaps with other people.

As another example imagine you're involved with someone in a relationship. You call this person every day and get together three or four nights a week. Something happens. He or she breaks a dinner date due to a purported family crisis. That evening, you get tired of sitting around alone so you go shopping at the mall. Lo and behold, you spot him or her arm-in-arm with a former flame going into the theatre. You are hurt and upset. So what is the most effective manner to convey your displeasure? Yes, you could call this person the next day and go crazy. Or you could wait until you get together again and bring up "something we need to talk about." On the other hand, perhaps the most effective mode of communication would be to say or do absolutely nothing. Don't be at those places where you might run into each other. Don't call the next night. Or the next. Use your answering machine to screen your calls. Be totally inaccessible for about a week. Isn't this communicating? You can feel the energy in the air.

And here's an example using your prospects and customers. You can't *not* communicate with them, either. Ask yourself: What are you communicating to them between calls? How does that person interpret the lack of a thank-you note? Or the lack of a telephone call between appointments, just to make sure all is well and to see if there's anything you can do to be helpful. Your failure to write or phone may *really* communicate that you're taking them for granted or that you have no interest in dealing with them unless you're out for a sale. That may not be what you intended to communicate. Thus, you must become consciously aware of what you communicate.

Keep all this in mind when you make up your weekly and daily plans. Sure, you've got sales calls to make. And phone calls to get those appointments. But what about everyone else? What are you communicating by *not* calling or writing them?

Here are some ideas. Get in the habit of sending a thank-you note when you get an order. Send your customers birthday cards and cards for holidays—St. Patricks Day, the Fourth of July, and Halloween. No, it's not something you *have* to do, but wouldn't you agree it communicates a more desirable message than doing nothing? And when you call between appointments, you'll get an interesting surprise. The customer will probably complain about something. It won't be anything major, otherwise he or she would have called you, but just some little problem or something not quite right. Is that bad? Not at all! Remember, a complaining customer is a happy customer. It's when they *stop* complaining that you need to be concerned, because that lack of communication should alert you that they may be ready to take their business elsewhere.

You just can't *not* communicate. Communication has no "off" switch.

# Secret 2:
# Communication Is a Flow of Sending and Receiving

Remember the traditional S–R model of communication from Psych 101? In that model, the two parties in the process are designated as Sender–Receiver or Stimulus–Response. Sender encodes a message which is decoded by the receiver. As long as there is no "noise" in the transmission to cause a misinterpretation of the message, the receiver gets the intended message and provides feedback, or the process reverses and the receiver now becomes the sender and the sender reverts to receiver.

Consider the traditional model and whether it's descriptive of interpersonal communication. Think it is? Let's take a closer look. Yes, the traditional model is good at describing one-way communication such as a radio or TV station, or even two-way radio, where the sender only speaks and the receiver only listens until the sender says "over," signifying a reversal of the process. But what about other communication modes, like when you're face-to-face with another person? Is that what's happening? A little too simplified, isn't it? When people interact, it's not one person just sending and the other just receiving. Remember, there's no "off" switch. You can't *not* communicate. Even when someone else is speaking, you continue to send messages nonverbally, such as "I see what you're driving at. That's a very important point, and I'm glad you brought it to my attention," or "I'm so bored. When can I get outta here?" or "Get on with it and shut up. *I* have something *important* to say!"

To be an effective communicator, you must be alert to continuously *receive* messages, even as you speak. When you speak, it's easy to fall into the trap of focusing only on yourself. That's a mistake. Remember, the other person doesn't have an "off" switch, either. As they listen, they're also *sending* messages. Can you afford to miss them?

Interpersonal communication, then, is more than just Send/ Receive —Switch—Receive/Send. It's a flow! All parties are *always* sending, *always* receiving, and continuously providing feedback and reinforcement. To be an effective communicator you need to get in that flow. Don't look at statements or gestures in isolation. Don't focus so much on what you're saying or planning to say next that you fail to pick up on cues which indicate where the flow is going in the mind of the prospect. Instead, concentrate on listening and observing.

Effective communication is a lot like being out on a river in a canoe. You know where you want to go, the goal of the sales call. If you consider only yourself and paddle directly to your goal, the flow of the current will take you somewhere else. But if you first sit back and observe where the flow is going, you can then adjust your speed and direction and wind up at your goal at the end of the journey.

Where you are at journey's end is what's important. Get in the flow!

# Secret 3:
# Use All Five Dimensions of Communication

So far, we've seen that communication is a continuous process that never stops, and that it's a simultaneous flow of stimulus, response, and reinforcement. But it's more. Communication has five different dimensions, and to be an effective communicator, you've got to tune into all five.

We've already touched on the first dimension: Sending plus receiving. For the second dimension, remember the magic word from Chapter 1. Listen! Unless you're so low on the assertiveness scale as to be bordering on submission, I suspect you share a problem common to most: You're a lot better at sending than receiving. In the remainder of this chapter, we'll address some specific points to help improve the receiving dimension of communication. That is the second dimension of communication: it can be either conscious or unconscious.

Combine the first two dimensions of communication and see what you've got. You can consciously send or unconsciously send, consciously receive or unconsciously receive. Isn't it logical that your communication effectiveness will be heightened if you enhance your conscious awareness of both incoming and outgoing messages?

For starters, we need to reduce or eliminate unconsciously sending *anything*. We must focus on all our verbal, nonverbal, and behavioral cues and consider how others may interpret the messages. Is this what we wish to convey? If not, the message needs to be consciously altered so that the other party perceives what it is we wish to send. Take a walk in their shoes and be aware of the impact of your message. If, for whatever reason, you wish to offend someone, go ahead, consciously do so. But there is no excuse for *un*consciously offending anyone.

Just as we need to be consciously aware of what we send, it's equally desirable to become more conscious of messages we receive. Think of these everyday situations. Someone you meet appears to be a nice person, but for some reason you have reservations about him or her. You're interviewing candidates for a job, and ten minutes into an interview you decide that this is the person you want to hire. Or a good-looking person asks you out, but you decline, sensing something uncool. Intuition? Perhaps. You hear a lot today about "intuitive management" and "going with your gut." It almost makes you believe that all sorts of valuable insights are coming out of nowhere. And to a certain extent they may be, but more likely, what you're calling "intuition" or "gut-feel" is really a result of messages you unconsciously received. Try this: Think about one of those experiences where "intuition" directed you for no apparent reason. Search for details. I'll bet there was something, or a series of things, which affected your thinking. It may have been something someone said or did which you didn't even notice at the time—some little thing like a person's voice, gestures, or eye movement. A communication cue you unconsciously received probably played a part in your "intuition." Now consider this: How many valuable communication cues are you missing altogether, consciously or unconsciously? Have you ever looked back at a situation and wondered why you hadn't seen something obviously going on right in front of you? Sure you have! Wake up, tune in, and become conscious of all the messages that are coming toward you, if only you're alert enough to pick up on them. When you develop the skill of being more conscious of what you send and what you receive, you will become a more effective communicator. And you'll also discover that when others are consciously communicating with you, their messages are usually very controlled to achieve their designated objective. By contrast, their unconscious messages aren't as specific and focused, but they may be even more useful in determining what's really going on.

This all brings us to the third dimension of communication: It can be either intentional or unintentional. At first, you may say that's synonymous with conscious or unconscious, but it isn't quite the same. You may be conscious of what you're communicating, but have you thought through your message to determine exactly what you wish to convey, and have you planned a series of communication cues to successfully generate the desired message? In Chapter Two, we saw how our activities need a plan. Well, so does communication. Intentionally determining what we wish to communicate and consciously going about doing so is called impression formation, the communication package. That will be discussed as the sixth secret in this chapter.

The last two dimensions of communication are closely intertwined, and I'll be discussing them in detail. The first of these is the content component of communication. The other is something you may not have thought about much, particularly if you're an analytic or a driver, low on sensitivity: Communication also consists of a relationship component. Your content may be impeccable—with all the right facts, all the facts right, beautifully presented in living color—but it's all for naught if the other party doesn't like and trust you. Content has to be right, of course, but so do relationships. To address that requires an understanding of the tools of the trade, including written, verbal, and nonverbal modes.

# Secret 4:
# Think About the Content Component

The content component of communication is what your brain's left hemisphere is concerned about. Thinking, logic, facts. If you're dealing with an analytic or a driver, this is the major focus of your presentation, of course. And even if you're selling to an amiable or an expressive, you still want to be sure your facts are appropriate and correct. You just won't need as many of them.

Generally, the content component of communication is most effectively conveyed by verbal or written means. Verbal and written communication have formal structure, language, and grammatical rules. It's not as easy to convey a specific and unambiguous message nonverbally, though I can think of a few circumstances when I have done so after an opposing driver performed an unanticipated maneuver.

If you're a business professional, or entertain any hope of ever becoming one, I hope and trust you appreciate the need for written and verbal communication skills. If you can't properly convey content, you're going to experience severe limitations. That's a fact and it is something you need to address head on. American business is conducted in Business English and if you don't speak it and write it properly, one of your "A" priorities for next year *must* be to enroll in programs and coursework to develop those skills. And you college graduates, don't think this doesn't apply to you. My personal experience has been that around 20 percent of college seniors majoring in business lack adequate writing, grammar, and spelling skills. Good thing for you most professors hate grading and thus use multiple choice exams. In the world of business, however, lack of those skills is a roadblock you won't get around.

I am reminded of the story of someone applying for a job who, on the employment application, was asked to describe herself in 100 words or less. Her response:

## Concise.

She got the job. Remember that word. Don't generate a 20-page report if you can say it all in three. In fact, if you can't say it in one page, remove some of your material from the document and attach it as an appendix. Why? Because most businesspeople will take the time to read a one-page memo and will look at appendices if the memo is of interest. But if it's over a page long, most businesspeople won't look at it at all. Or they'll shuffle it over someplace where they'll look at it when they have enough time. And you know what that means. They won't look at it at all.

Also, be aware of certain words guaranteed to kill a sale, and avoid them. Like "sign" and "contract." You never sign a contract, you initial an agreement. Or "cost" and "expense." There are no costs and expenses, there are investments. The initial investment is X and the monthly investment is Y. You don't have someone "buy." You let them "have" or "own." There are no "problems," only points to be addressed.

When discussing expenses, speak in smaller time periods. When discussing profits, speak of longer time periods. An expense, or shall I say an investment, of $30 a month is "only a dollar a day," whereas a profit of $30 a month is "$365 a year." Little numbers for expenses; big numbers for profits.

My final point on content is the most important. Grammar and spelling have got to be right, but that's the easy part. And it's not enough. Whether you're writing a memo, a proposal, or a book, it's also essential that facts be organized and connected in a logical sequence. The same is true for a speech or presentation. Start off by outlining what you're going to cover, in the form of an agenda or table of contents. Then cover it. Finally, summarize or highlight the most important points. Or, to be concise:

Tell 'em what you're going to tell 'em; tell 'em; and tell 'em what you told 'em.

# Secret 5:
# The Relationship Component Is the Key Factor

We went through the content component of communication pretty fast, didn't we? Thinking, logic, and what it "is." Unfortunately, it won't be quite as easy to get through the next component, relationship. This is the stuff your right brain hemisphere is all about—feelings, likes, dislikes. Feelings and relationships are by their very nature difficult to quantify and thus do not lend themselves to precise observation and evaluation. Contributing to that is the dominant role played by nonverbal communication in relationships and feelings. No formal structure, language, and rules. We can't take an individual message in isolation, out of context, and determine its meaning. And it will take a lot longer to cover the relationship component because it has to do with the nature of the human animal. The truth is, we generally do not act according to logic, thinking, and facts. We more frequently make decisions on the basis of emotions and feelings. Most of the remainder of this chapter will address the relationship component for one simple reason: In selling, as in all human interaction, it's the most important factor. If it feels good, people will do it, and then develop logical and rational justifications for their actions. If it doesn't feel right, no logical factual arguments will change their minds. Have you ever tried to get a faith healer to document results and compare them to the demonstrated efficacy of medical treatments? Or given someone logical facts to persuade him or her to like a person he or she didn't care for? It doesn't work.

Does this come as a surprise to you? Or, if it's not a surprise, do you tend to think that others may act on whim, emotions, and feelings, but that you are a bastion of thinking and logic? Let's face it, we've all been conditioned to believe that the best way to make decisions is to rationally weigh the pros, cons, and options. In our society, feelings and emotions have historically been of secondary importance. Recently, I've been seeing a lot more books and articles addressing the benefits of less structure and organization with more feelings and creativity in decision-making. Good. Pure logic and thinking may be the way things are done on Vulcan, but not here.

If you still aren't comfortable with the idea that you, like everyone else, are primarily driven by nonrational feelings and emotions, ask yourself a few  things. Last time you fell in love, was it a logical, rational choice in which you procured all available pertinent information before you selected that person, or were you suddenly thrust into a condition of temporary insanity? Or how about when you bought your house and car? Yes, you may have shopped around a bit and compared data; but I'll still bet that unless you're an analytic, the one you bought was the one you looked at and felt "I want it." Facts and figures just came in later when you wanted to justify the reasoned logic of your decision.

Consider advertising. There are still a few people who sit in ivory towers believing in consumer behavior decision-making models. They believe that the major role of advertising is to persuade you to make a purchase decision. Information input to a rational process. By contrast, others contend that the major role of advertising is to reinforce satisfaction with brands already bought, to give the customer rational justification for their decision. Who's right? Who knows? But I tend to agree more with the latter perspective. Advertising, selling—they're the same. Facts and logic will only get you so far. Relationships and emotions are the keys to success in selling. Let's repeat that:

# RELATIONSHIPS AND EMOTIONS ARE THE KEYS TO SUCCESS IN SELLING

Effective communication in salesmanship requires an understanding of the relationship component above all else. So, let's take a good look at relationship, exploring two major points.

# People Buy from Salespeople They Like and Trust

Let's add to that: People give referrals to salespeople they like and trust. We've touched on this point in the first chapters. Customers like and trust salespeople who focus on them, their needs, and their interests; who do what they say they'll do; who demonstrate competence, sincerity, and appreciation. Salespeople with ethical behavior command respect and display integrity.

We also know that people are constantly defining the nature of their relationship. In the environment all living things are growing or they're dying. This is true for you as a person. If you stop growing, you start dying. Relationships are the same—vibrant and growing, or stagnant and dying. You're building trust and respect or you're losing it. You're drawing closer together or drifting further apart. All your relationships are in a state of continual flux and change. You can't not communicate.

# Power and Assertiveness Are Always Being Played Out in Any Communication

You are in a position of superiority, inferiority, or equality at any given moment, and these positions are continuously changing and being tested. I'll talk about power and negotiation applications in detail in Chapter Six, but here I'm going to discuss the dynamics of power in relational communication.

Obviously, you would love to have a superior power position in any situation. If not, if you'd really rather be at the mercy of others in an inferior position, please put this book down now, go to the phone, dial 911, and tell them you need professional help. Unfortunately, in selling—as in life—we are seldom in a position of dominance and control. Yes, occasionally the phone will ring and someone will say, "We're running out of three-eighths-inch carbon steel widgets and you're the only supplier who meets our specifications. Can you air freight us ten million of them by Monday? Price is no object. Can we pay you cash in advance?" Enjoy such moments when you may. There aren't going to be too many of them.

Sure, you aren't going to be in a superior power position all that often. On the other hand, there's no reason for you to automatically assume an inferior position, either. But think about it: How often do you go into a sales call believing that you need the order more than they need your product? That your competitors have products that are as good or better and will beat your price? How often do you ask someone out believing that he or she really doesn't have as much of a need for you as the need you feel for them, and that someone else would probably show him or her a better time? I'm sure that's happened to you, just as it's happened to me and everyone else I know. If, however, such assumptions continue to dog you on a regular basis, maybe it's time to reassess.

Selling—a product or yourself—is built on a foundation of mutual benefit. I win. You win. We conduct a business or social transaction because it's in our enlightened self-interest to do so. It all comes back to what we were saying about features and benefits. If you have no benefits to offer, don't waste your time calling anyone. They have no reason to deal with you. By contrast, if you've done your homework—and know everything there is to know about your product, customer, competition, and industry—it's very likely that you'll have identified features of unique benefit to your customer. Things they want! Things they need!

Then, there's no reason or excuse for making a call in an inferior power position.

You should enter the selling situation with no less than equality in power and assertiveness. You test them, they test you. Your objective is to maintain an adult–adult, win–win dialogue throughout the process, and that should happen if the other party reciprocates in your spirit of respect and fairness. However, unless you still believe in Santa Claus and the Easter Bunny, you surely do not expect and demand fairness in life. In many situations the other party will attempt to improve their prospects by diminishing your power position. Watch out for the two tactics commonly used to do this.

The first tactic is role playing. Instead of communicating with you on an adult–adult level, the other party will play either a parental or child role. In the parental role they will convey an image of an all-knowing parent speaking down to the child. Their objective is to diminish your power by convincing you that they are more knowledgeable than you and that you can't get along without them. If, like a good little boy or girl, you behave properly—say, by making a significant unilateral concession—they might "do something for you." Otherwise, no dinner tonight. Here's an example:

| | |
|---|---|
| You: | ". . . so that's what I'm recommending." |
| Customer: | "It's interesting. But I know that the buying committee will object to some of the provisions." |
| You: | "They will?" |
| Customer: | "Yes. For instance, you're charging $100 a unit for shipping, but your competitor only charges $75." |
| You: | "That's true, but they only ship to the terminal. We deliver to your door." |
| Customer: | "I know that. But the committee just sees an extra $25. I'm just trying to help you out. Let me show you how to change this proposal so the committee might consider it." |
| You: | "I'd appreciate that very much." |
| Customer: | "All right. Let's look at your price: It's $300 higher per unit than the competition." |
| You: | "Yes, but remember that our quality and features are far superior. Over the long run, we'll cost you far less." |

| | |
|---|---|
| Customer: | "I believe that, but the committee will only see the extra $300. So if you drop your price $300, that obstacle is out of the way, isn't it?" |
| You: | "Well, yes." |
| Customer: | "And when it's time to reorder they'll know that your higher price is justified, won't they?" |
| You: | "I guess so." |
| Customer: | "See why that's better? One thing you'll learn in selling is that the reorder is what counts. Take a little less on the first order." |
| You: | "That makes sense." |
| Customer: | "Another thing. You've specified 2 percent/10, Net 30, and a 2 percent per month extra charge past 30 days. You don't ever want to do that." |
| You: | "I don't?" |
| Customer: | "No. You're saying I have to pay within 10 days to get the 2 percent discount. Paperwork usually takes 14 to 21 days in a company like ours. See how that could be an inconvenience?" |
| You: | "Would it?" |
| Customer: | "Oh, yes, it could upset all our accounting procedures. The way to handle it is to give us the 2 percent discount off the top and make it Net 30." |
| You: | "But if we cut the price and the shipping costs, I don't think we can go another 2 percent." |
| Customer: | "Oh, go ahead. What's a lousy 2 percent? One more thing, though. You don't ever want to specify an extra charge past 30 days for a customer like us. Take that out." |
| You: | "Why?" |
| Customer: | "The committee looks at that and figures you think we're a bunch of deadbeats. Is that how you feel?" |
| You: | "Oh, no, not at all." |
| Customer: | "Then you don't need it in there. And something else I think would help you. . ." |

And so forth and so forth. In such a situation, if they sense your submission to the parental role, your cause is lost.

The other extreme of role playing is the child role. Here the other party yells, screams, rants, and raves just like all the children I see with their parents at the neighborhood Food World twice a week when I'm trying to do my grocery shopping. Playing the child role succeeds in either of two ways:

(1) The other party concedes something in hopes of buying her way out of the tantrum; or

(2) The other party reverts to the child role himself, in which case he's been brought down to the initiator's level.

A variation of the child role power game is one-upsmanship. Here, someone assumes dominance through a series of statements calculated to be equal to or more assertive than the other party's responses. Friends, acquaintances, and lovers play at this all the time. When I'm out with a group of people and taking a momentary interlude between periods of pseudo-intellectual conversation, I love to tune in on the one-upsmanship games. You can even keep score. A dominant power statement gets a +1. A neutral statement gets a zero. And a submissive statement gets a −1. For instance:

> Jon:   "I'm going to the party tonight." (Dominant statement: +1)
>
> Jim:   "See you later. I'm going to the bar." (Dominant statement: +1. Net for the exchange: Tie.)

But this might happen:

> Jon:   "I'm going to the party tonight." (+1)
>
> Jim:   "I'm not sure what I'm going to do." (Neutral statement: 0. Net for the exchange: +1 in favor of Jon.)

Or even this:

> Jon:   "I'm going to the party tonight." (+1)
>
> Jim:   "Do you think I could go with you?" (Submissive statement: −1. Net for the exchange: +2 in favor of Jon.)

You keep track of a series of such exchanges to ascertain the ebb and flow of the power exchange. To continue the last example:

Jon:    "Hell, no. I don't want you around." (+1)

Jim:    "But I won't be any bother." (–1)

       Round 2: +2 for Jon.

Jon:    "I said no. Get lost!" (+1)

Jim:    "Well, all right. I guess I'll just go over to Dave's place." (0)

       Round 3: +1 for Jon.

Jon:    "What's going on over there?" (0)

Jim:    "None of your damn business!" (+1)

Aha! The worm has turned! Round 4 goes +1 for Jim and Jon's overall lead is down to +4.

I've found that the most interesting games are those which start off with a long series of ties. Then it all comes down to see who can take just one round and win the game.

A:    "I saw that!" (+1)

B:    "You saw *what*?" (+1)

       Round 1: 0.

A:    "Who you were just talking to. You didn't think I saw you, did you?" (+1)

B:    "I don't give a damn whether you saw me or not. I'll talk to anybody I please." (+1)

       Round 2: 0.

A:    "Sure. And let me sit here alone. I don't know why you even brought me." (+1)

B:    "I'll tell you why I brought you. I brought you because I get all lonely inside if I don't have someone to nag at me every 15 minutes." (+1)

       Round 3: 0

I'm sure you've heard an exchange like that. Or the variation of the theme, in which case the series of ties continues until someone manages to lose.

A:   "I really would like to see you." (–1)

B:   "You still want to see *me?*" (–1)

Round 1: 0.

A:   "I know I haven't been very considerate lately." (–1)

B:   "Oh, no. It's nothing you've done." (–1)

Round 2: 0. Getting to be a bit much, isn't it?

A:   "I don't know why you put up with me." (–1)

B:   "I guess I just can't do without you." (–1)

Yuk! I can't stand any more of that. But you get the idea. You may have always considered power in the context of an organizational or negotiation scenario. However, power and assertiveness are present in any communication. No, I am not advocating that you attempt to dominate every person you meet and every conversation you have. Human communication flourishes best at an adult–adult level with neutral power statements. Just be aware of how the power game is playing out, and don't let anyone dominate *you*. Naturally, if the other party wants to be dominated, you may wish to accommodate them. On the other hand, if the other party wants to be dominated, you also might refuse. That way, you'd *really* be dominating them.

# Secret 6:
# Consciously Control Your Impression Formation

Impression formation is the conscious control of all your communication cues, written, verbal, and nonverbal. It means packaging those cues to convey yourself as a professional, competent adult. A winner. Doing those things we've already discussed in the first three chapters is part of creating that impression. Here I'd like to look at four more parts of the package.

# (1) Don't Make Mistakes

You can do 99 things right and one thing wrong, and what do you think people are going to remember? Of course. The one thing you did wrong. If you don't believe me, just ask Richard Nixon or General Custer. This includes all communication cues, particularly things like mispronouncing or misspelling someone's name or other germane item. Recall your reaction the last time a salesperson spelled your name wrong. It didn't nudge you toward the close, did it?

Particularly with analytics, but also with drivers, don't have inaccurate facts and information; or typos; or unsubstantiated personal opinions in lieu of facts. Be on time. Don't make a nonverbal faux pas such as being the only person at the dinner dressed too casually. Yes, you want to stand out, but not that way.

# (2) Impression Formation Is Predominantly Nonverbal

Impressions are relational in nature, and as we've discussed, the relational component of communication is most effectively conveyed nonverbally. There are several excellent books on nonverbal communication. Let me just touch on a few thoughts which you may not encounter elsewhere.

I'd like to share my opinion about attire. I know the dress for success books are very specific: Wool suit, dark blue or charcoal grey, never brown, and so forth. Well, I can't wear wool. Even a wool sport coat, which isn't even touching my skin, will have me itching within moments. Sure, you want to look good, but not at the price of being uncomfortable. If a particular type of clothing is either uncomfortable to you or you just don't like it, wear something else. Some occupations—bankers, lawyers—and some companies—IBM—aren't very flexible on dress codes. If that creates a problem for you, take up a new occupation or go work for someone else.

Brown can look good. Slacks and a matching sport coat can look good. If it's tasteful, good quality, and well within the bounds of the respective organizational culture, I say wear it. Don't just be a corporate clone, wearing what everyone else does just because everyone else does. Establish your own style, within limits, of course. Consider appropriateness and the norms of those you're calling on. The latest thing in Italian suits looks great in New York, but doesn't cut it in Montgomery.

As far as accessories go, do what's right for you, but also be aware of the impressions they convey. If you have a briefcase, have a new one and a good one. Most major companies will foot the bill as part of office supplies. I know you're supposed to wear a thin gold watch with a matching band. I don't. I have a Bulova Accutron Space–View that I bought new in 1971. It's big and bulky, but I like it. I've had it overhauled three times because I have yet to see another watch I'd rather have. Now it's started to become something of a collector's item, but I don't care.

The less jewelry the better, and the less fragrance the better. Under fragrance I include everything from cologne to scented deodorant. Particularly for men, but also for women, the less of a smell you exude the better. I don't care if your boyfriend or girlfriend gave you a bottle of this stuff for your birthday and he or she just loves it. Leave it at home. In business, you don't want your scent to arrive ahead of your handshake. You may think you "only use a little" and that others would hardly notice. But your nose may be used to it and have turned off the sensory message to your brain.

Avoid wearing anything that identifies you with any belief, political persuasion, or organization. Your business purpose is business, not social persuasion. That includes bumper stickers on your car. Neither "Re-elect the President" nor "Impeach the President" is appropriate, not on you and not on your car in the customer's parking lot. I trust you will not call on a prospect wearing a button that says "Down with all capitalist pigs." Similarly, I would avoid college rings. You may be proud of your Georgia Tech ring, but your customer, who played football at Georgia, may not be impressed. This is also applicable to religious artifacts. You may feel that gold cross in your lapel is a testimonial to your faith but your prospect may belong to a different religion or perceive you to be a right-wing radical attempting to impose your views. Such artifacts may detract attention from your business purpose, as well as cause a negative reaction. Remember Point 1: Don't make mistakes. If you absolutely, positively cannot separate your personal, political, social, and organizational affiliations from business, you might consider a different line of work.

A quick one-liner on other aspects of nonverbal communication in impression formation: Look alive! Above all else, show enthusiasm. Over the years, I've dealt with dozens of recruiters for major companies, and time after time they've told me that one factor was paramount in their hiring decision. No, not grade point average, extracurricular activities. or attire. Yes, enthusiasm. You've had similar experiences. If a salesperson has genuine and sincere enthusiasm about his or her product, it's contagious. You're more interested in hearing what they have to say, and you're more likely to buy. But if a salesperson lacks enthusiasm and drones along in the presentation, it turns you off. If they're not sold, you won't be, either.

Use nonverbal communication to form an impression of alertness and enthusiasm. Stand up straight. Walk with a positive assertiveness. Look your prospect in the eye and offer a firm handshake, not a limp fish. Make use of gestures to enforce important points.

Naturally, the verbal content of your speech has got to be right, with proper grammar and pronunciation, and factors organized and presented in a logical sequence. *How* you speak falls under the domain of nonverbal communication, and it's no less important. First, don't speak too fast—stay around 120 to 150 words per minute. It's not easy to do. In any person-to-person meeting or in a presentation, you're under stress. Stress tends to speed up your rate of speech. Remember in school when you had to make a 15-minute presentation? You rehearsed it the night before to 15 minutes exactly. Then you made the presentation in class, and guess what? That's right, eight minutes flat. You were under stress and rolling along between 250 and 300 words per minute. Think about that when you talk to prospects, face-to-face or on the phone. Slow down!

Also, don't be a monotone. Vary volume and pitch, use pauses and gestures to emphasize important points, and maintain positive eye contact. Eyes are the most important nonverbal communication channel for defining and establishing relationships and feelings. Read the messages in your prospect's eyes to determine whether you're connecting or not.

If there's one thing *not* to do in speaking, that would be the use of nonfluencies such as "um" or the perennial favorite, "you know." Studies have indicated that you are 47 percent more likely to suffer a "you know" addiction if you went to a school that had a football team or if you like to watch pregame interviews on "Lead-off Man" or "The NFL Today." It has always astonished me how otherwise intelligent people appear unable to get through a basic sentence without interjecting at least two or three "you knows" to spice things up. You know what the literal translation for "you know" is, you know. Well, you know, the literal translation for "you know" is, simply: "Duh." So why do people say "you know"? It's a pause filler. You're running along in a sentence, finish one thought, and your head needs a quarter second to organize the next thought. Rather than pause for a fraction of a second, you bridge with a "you know." How about you? How often do you come out with "you knows"? If you suffer this affliction you're probably not even aware of it, so you'd better ask someone else.

In business you are permitted one "you know" per day. In a job interview, just one may have you out the door. If you have a "you know" speech defect—and it *is* a speech defect—you've got to get rid of it now. Make it an "A" priority. There's only one way: Every time you come out with a "you know," you must stop, pause, and say "Duh." You might want to wait until the weekend to start this. I assure you, three or four times humiliating yourself with a "Duh" and you'll start watching out for the "you knows."

# (3) What You See Is Not What *They* See

Psychologists call this selective perception. People tend to see what they want and expect to see and filter things through their own value systems and experiences. If they expect to see roses, they probably will. If they expect garbage, same thing. Another side to that equation: People tend to see and seek in others those things which they are themselves. I've noticed this at the elegant parties to which I'm so often invited. If, in a room of 100 people, there are six golfers, those six golfers will be standing around talking to each other within a half hour. Play this to your advantage. Be alert, and see and seek areas of common ground with your prospect to build rapport and relationship.

# (4) Take a Look at Yourself

Before reading further, please put this book down and remove all your clothes. I don't care where you are, just do it. Now, stand in front of a mirror and rate yourself on a scale of 1 to 10. How well are you doing with what you've got? What do you weigh compared to a 24-year-old of your height who's in shape? And what do you weigh compared to what *you* weighed at 24? You should weigh no more today than you did at 24. That assumes, of course, that you were in shape at 24. If you were out of shape at 24, and that was more than ten years ago, I'll bet you are a sight to behold today. Too often I see people in their twenties, thirties, and forties who provoke me to ask myself: How can this person stand being so out of shape? Doesn't he or she miss being able to see all ten toes? But I don't see too many people like that in their fifties and beyond. You know why.

I don't mean to be cruel. It just comes down to this: You can do everything else right in verbal and nonverbal communication and still make a negative impression if you're physically out of shape. I know that's not fair, but life isn't fair, remember? True, shaping up is a lot easier for some people than for others. I'm lucky. I don't gain weight if I maintain a diet of fruit, salad, veggies, one entree a day, absolutely no snacks, and run 33 miles a week. It may not be that easy for you. When you are in shape, you look better, feel better, and live longer. Exercise makes you less tired, not more. It's a boost to self-esteem. You create a stronger impression which can't help but enhance prospects for success. You're also going to be considerably less stressed out. Business, and particularly sales, is stressful. You need an outlet.

If the shoe fits, wear it. No more ice cream cones, cashews, and cake; no candy bars or chips between meals; at the very least, a two–mile brisk walk every day. No time? Make time! Get up 30 minutes earlier and do it.

# Summing Up

That's our look at the Six Top Secrets of Communication. To review:

- **Secret 1:** There's no "off" switch. You can't *not* communicate. The *lack* of a message *is* a message. If you're not following up calls on your prospects, if you're not sending cards and thank-you notes, you may be conveying that you're taking their business for granted or just don't care. Keep in touch.

- **Secret 2:** Get in the flow of communication, simultaneously sending messages and actively listening. The other person can't not communicate, either. Can you afford to miss the messages they're sending you by being so busy running your mouth that you fail to observe and listen?

- **Secret 3:** Tune into all five dimensions of communication. We must be conscious of everything we and others send and be sure we're sending the messages we intend to send.

- **Secret 4:** The content component of communication. We must have a solid base of correct facts and rational, logical thought.

- **Secret 5:** Deal with relationships and emotion. We all pride ourselves on being logical and rational, but we aren't.

- **Secret 6:** Conscious control of the image we project for impression formation. This includes understanding and utilizing all communication cues to achieve our objectives.

# CHAPTER 4

# Identifying and Developing Prospects

---

# The Five Top Secrets of Prospecting and Preparation

We've built the foundation. Now it's time to get out and do something. And the first thing we've got to do is to determine who it is we're going to sell to. So, who ya gonna call? This chapter addresses the Five Top Secrets of Prospecting and Preparation for the call.

The first secret is to be sure your prospects are qualified prospects. If you're spinning your wheels wasting time with people who aren't qualified to buy, you're in for long hours and small paychecks. Identifying prospects means generating lists of candidates who might be able to benefit from your product or service. This includes building referrals and finding pre-qualified prospects. Then, once you've determined which prospects you want to meet in person, you'll need to know the secrets of getting the appointment and preparing your sales presentation.

# Secret 1: Qualification Is the Key

To understand prospecting, think of a pyramid. At the lowest level you have a large number of suspects. At the top there are a few qualified prospects with whom you get an appointment. Effective prospecting involves narrowing down suspects in two steps. First, you have to determine whether the suspect is a prospect; that is, whether that person is a candidate for enjoying the benefits of your product or service. Then, you must ascertain whether a prospect is a qualified prospect; that is, whether that person is in the financial position to pay for your product or service. Let's look at this example. You're a car salesperson with a list of five names, addresses, and phone numbers. All suspects. Checking them out, you discover that one of your suspects is 13 years old and another is 93, has never had a license, and is confined to a nursing home. Two suspects that are not prospects. The other three are licensed drivers between the ages of 25 and 55: Prospects. One of these, age 25, has a take-home income of $1,000 a month with monthly obligations of $1,200. Although this person would probably love a new car, he or she can't afford the payments. There is no way you'll get the loan approved, so this is not a qualified prospect. One of your other prospects is 40 and fully qualified, but just took delivery of a new car. Qualified, yes, but not in the market at this time. The last prospect is 55, has an income of

$80,000 a year, no debts, and buys a new car every three years. The last one was 2½ years ago. Tell me: Who ya gonna call? Where do you want to spend your selling time?

Always remember to focus your selling time on qualified prospects who are ready to buy. If they're not qualified or not currently in the market, you need to uncover that fact in the least possible time, and politely move on. Let's face it, most suspects will not turn out to be qualified prospects. Depending on your business, maybe as few as one in ten. If it takes you as little as 15 minutes to qualify someone, that would mean it's taking you 2½ hours to uncover one qualified prospect. If you manage to get an appointment with one of three qualified prospects, that means it would take you one full day to procure one appointment. If, heaven forbid, you schedule an appointment without qualifying the prospect first, you might spend half a day, rather than 15 minutes, discovering their inability to buy. At that rate, you're making a presentation to a qualified prospect once a week. How many of those are you going to close? Enough to cover expenses?

Sure, qualifying can be awkward, particularly with individuals. You need to ask some very specific questions about personal finances. That can be uncomfortable, both for you and your prospect. We tend to avoid things which are uncomfortable. We hope they'll go away. Unfortunately, the financial condition of an individual or corporation isn't something that will go away if we ignore it. You must address it up front, but discreetly.

Let's start with qualifying corporations, where some of what you need may already be in the public domain. The annual report and income statement may be available at your local public library or direct from the company upon request. If you deal with such corporations, you might consider buying one or more shares of their stock. Then, you'll receive those reports automatically.

If you've suffered through one or more courses in economics or finance, you know to beware of annual reports and income statements. Those accountants can hide a lot of dirty laundry between the lines, bless their little analytic hearts. Check out the bond ratings services through your library or stockbroker and remember that a "B" does not mean better than average.

You may be surprised at how valuable the industry grapevine is at identifying companies in trouble. Attend conventions, trade shows, or meetings of industry associations, and keep your eyes and ears open. Should an inordinate number of a company's sales and marketing people be testing the waters for alternative opportunities, you might wish to investigate further.

This may come as a shock to you, but many companies, even healthy ones, don't pay their bills on time, or at all. Again, the industry grapevine may be more helpful than any published source at identifying such organizations. No, it's not fair, but some companies will give you a nice order and accept a shipment or two. When you diplomatically ask them to please expedite payment, they may send you a little something, but not as much as the price of the next shipment you're sending. When you finally reach the point that you will not increase their line of credit further, and insist they make a payment of at least as much as the value of the next delivery, they cease paying you altogether. Then they go out and find another supplier to start the process anew. If your paycheck is in any way affected by your company's ability to collect payment for its products and services, you might want to know about such tactics in advance and, as part of the qualifying process, underscore a policy of cash on delivery. If they balk at that, thank them and save yourself the time you'd have wasted on a sales call.

With individuals, information may be available from syndicated sources, banks, mortgage companies, and accounts with whom they currently have credit. Individuals will put most of this information on a credit application for you, so all your credit department has to do is check it out. The problem is that by the time they finally fill out the credit application, you may have already invested three or four hours establishing rapport, making your presentation/demonstration, and closing the sale. If you're in a business like real estate, you may have killed three or four days. Clearly, you can't afford to waste that kind of time on anyone who isn't a qualified prospect. So right up front, you've got to ask qualifying questions. If you can eliminate them in two minutes, don't take ten. And if you just can't bring yourself to qualifying them before getting into your presentation, you may want to consider getting out of sales and into social work.

Effective qualifying means asking caring involvement questions and carefully listening to the responses. It can be subtle, with the prospect not even aware that he or she is being qualified. Initial questions like "What are you driving now?"/"Have you had it since it was new?"/"Did you finance it with GMAC?" or "What room would you be putting this in?"/"How large is that room?"/"What other kinds of furniture and accessories do you have in that room?" may, at the outset, give you clues as to whether you have an unqualified looker or a serious qualified prospect. Then, opening qualifying questions should give you an idea of what that person does for a living, and where and how long they've been employed. If they're married, someone else may be involved in the decision. You may have to sell two people, not one. If they have kids, it may affect the type of product best suited to them. If they have a lot of kids, they may not have enough discretionary income to qualify for anything at all.

If you're dealing in big-ticket items, you have to be even more direct and specific. You have to steer them toward the Cavalier if they can't afford the Corvette. The brick ranch instead of the estate on the lake. In circumstances like this, if they pass the opening qualification questions, proceed immediately to obtaining information on income and obligations. Not in a threatening manner, of course. Explain to them that you can help them organize information that will help them make decisions, and information they'll need regardless of what they buy from whom. Be caring and helpful. Don't seem as though you're conducting the Inquisition. But get right down to determining what kind of payments they can afford, how large a loan they're qualified for, and the maximum sales price that translates to. Failing to do so just wastes your time and theirs. Not a good example of effective time management, is it?

# Secret 2:
# Build a Base of Suspects

It's simple: Before you can sell to anyone, you've got to find someone to sell to. And to do that, you've got to generate a substantial list of suspects from which you will produce a target list of qualified prospects to meet in person. If you're a salesperson in a retail showroom, you may think this does not apply to you. It does. If all you do is wait around at your place of business for customers to come to you, you're an order-taker, not a salesperson. Order-takers usually earn about 20 percent more than the kids flipping burgers at McDonald's.

There's a name for this process of generating lists of suspects and seeking appointments with those who turn out to be qualified prospects. It's called cold-call prospecting. Kind of sends a shiver up your spine, doesn't it? The words "cold-call prospecting" usually evoke about the same response as "root canal," "nuclear winter," or "IRS audit." Most salespeople hate and/or dread cold-calling prospecting. The odds of any one suspect blooming into an appointment with a qualified prospect range between low and remote. You will experience rejection, perhaps bordering on hostility. Just don't take it personally. You're only a convenient someone for them to yell at. They don't even know you, so how can they hate you? The fact is, cold-call prospecting is something you have to do and it works if, first, you have a plan, and then, you have the discipline to put that plan into action. Let's look at several points about building that base of suspects.

# (1) Use the Resources of Your Company

Many companies will provide you lists of suspects or prospects. Use them. Ask your co-workers about their experiences. Seek suggestions from anyone and everyone who has gone before you. Learn from others what seems to work in your industry and how to go about doing it. Remember: You don't have to make *every* mistake anyone else has ever made.

Your company may have pieces of direct mail available for you at little to no cost. They may have training or techniques on how to go about prospecting and getting appointments. Look them over. Modify them as necessary to reflect your style.

Consider this: Particularly early on in a job, before the sales start rolling in and you're busting your quotas every month, your willingness to do what it takes in cold-call prospecting will demonstrate to your sales manager that you've got what it takes to be successful. Sales managers like that, because it makes *them* look good. And sales managers can be very helpful toward employees who make them look good.

# (2) Check Something out at the Library

Start by checking out the librarian. By definition, librarians are amiables with a touch of analytic thrown in. And they can help you locate the myriad of prospecting resources at the local public or university library—everything from *Dun and Bradstreet* to *Standard and Poor's*. Do you want big companies or small companies? Do you want all the companies related to a particular industry? Do you want all the companies that advertise? Do you want their address, phone number, and the name of the vice president of marketing? It's probably at the library, so get to know a librarian, tell him or her what you do, and the types of prospects you're looking for. Then, let that person guide you through the source material. While you're there, allow an extra hour or two to peruse the reference section on your own. It's all there waiting for you to discover it.

# (3) Check out the Phone Book

Depending on your business, go through the residential listings, the Yellow Pages, or the white business pages. Many libraries also have phone books for various cities. If not, or if it's more convenient, call the phone company. For a nominal charge, they'll send you just about any directory from just about anywhere in about 10–14 days. And they'll put the charge on your phone bill. If you regularly conduct business outside the area covered by your local phone company, those out-of-town phone books can be an invaluable resource of names, addresses, and numbers of potential prospects.

# (4) Check out the Other Phone Books

These include business-to-business directories and club and company rosters. If you're in Atlanta, would it be helpful for you to have a listing of all the names and titles of the employees at Georgia–Pacific or the Coca–Cola Company? If you're in Rochester, how about Kodak? Or if you're in Tuscaloosa, the University of Alabama? If you're targeting prospects in the upper income brackets, how about the membership list from the local country clubs or yacht clubs? Chances are you can't just call these clubs and companies and have them fire the list off to you. They're funny about things like that. But the lists are out there, and someone you know might have access to them.

Also consider reverse directories—organized by street address rather than alphabetically; membership lists of apartment or condominium homeowners associations; mailing lists and other syndicated lists of current and past users of related products. When you joined that CD club, did you wonder why ten other clubs wrote you? You were on a list. When you bought something through a catalogue, what happened? How about when you dialed that 800 number to order the belly buster?

The point is, companies and individual salespeople use syndicated lists because they're a source of good, probably qualified prospects with a demonstrated buying history. Maybe one or more would be a valuable resource for you or your company.

# (5) Check out the Service Department

Consider this example. When are you most receptive to buying a car? Is it on a day when you're happily enjoying miles and miles of carefree holiday driving? Hardly! It's the day when you have to get up an hour early to be in line at the service department. The service department opens at 7:30 A.M. Unless you want to stand around until 9:00 while they write up all the people in line ahead of you, you'd better get there 45 minutes to an hour early.

You may think the sales department opens at 9:00 A.M. In reality, the sales department opened at 6:30 A.M., when the first car arrived at the service door. That person sat there for an hour, listening to drive-time radio and wishing he or she had remembered to bring a book or newspaper. What if, just what if, a salesperson had been there to invite them into the showroom, where a fresh pot of coffee was on the brew? That salesperson might close more sales, before any other salespeople arrive, than anyone else does all day.

Do you sell televisions, stereos, or any other item which requires occasional—and expensive—service? Check out your service department and/or establish a relationship with independent service contractors. When the TV repair person gives them the bad news, he or she can also hand them your card and tell them to look you up for the best deal on a new set. They don't do so for free, of course, but instead use a technique called birddawging, which I'll go into in the next segment.

How about what you sell? Are there people having work done in a service department who are ready to buy something new or improved? Check out that service department and give it a little service yourself.

# (6) Check out the Government

And check out the Chamber of Commerce or related agencies and bureaus. Do they correspond with current or prospective businesses? Do they issue permits and licenses? You might discover that the permit and license stage is the optimal time for a sales call. By the time they open the doors for business, it may be too late.

All governmental agencies generate huge amounts of information and data. In my opinion, since they don't produce anything tangible, it's the only way they can justify stealing about 40 percent of the wages from all the productive working people in the country. You're paying for all that paperwork they're generating, so take advantage of it. Start by asking what agencies and bureaus deal with the industries and firms which might be prospects for you. Then uncover what information they have, its accessibility to you, and the procedures for getting it. Be persistent. Make some friends in the system.

# (7) Stake out a Territory

Do you belong to any groups, clubs, or professional associations? Are there people that you regularly see for work or pleasure? Then stake your claim on that group and make sure that everyone there knows what you sell. In and around your community that means getting involved in the school parents' association, youth activities, service organizations, industry and trade groups. And you may be interested in environmental, political, or religious organizations. Any time, any place that people who are potential prospects get together, you be there. Pass out those business cards so that everyone in the territory knows who you are, who you represent, what you sell, and how to contact you. Depending on your industry, trade shows and conventions can also be a golden opportunity to prospect, network, or share information.

One final item about staking out a territory—and it is so simple it's easy to forget: get out and walk or drive around. Take a different route than usual when you're on the road. Walk in, around, and through the mall or office complex. I'm sure there are some tenants you didn't know were there.

# (8) Have a Swapping Party

The type of swapping party I'm talking about is when you get together with salespeople in related but non-competing fields to swap leads. For example, a good group might be a real estate agent, an appraiser, a mortgage banker, and an insurance salesperson.

There are some guidelines on swapping parties. First, hold them regularly at a day and time convenient to everyone, perhaps Monday mornings for an early breakfast or Tuesday for lunch. Second, participants are expected to attend and are expected to bring leads to exchange with the others. If one of the members misses meetings too often and/or doesn't bring good leads to the party, delete that person and find someone else.

## (9) Pass out Those Business Cards

Every time you sit beside someone, give them a card and tell them what you do. Pass out cards every time you're standing in line, whether it's for buying a ticket for the movies or waiting for the gates to open at the ball game; every time you meet another person when you're shopping or browsing; and especially, every time you conduct a transaction with someone who is on the receiving end of *your* money: the butcher, the baker, the candlestick maker. Make sure they know who you are and the products, services, and benefits you provide. What are the probabilities of one of those business cards ever leading to a sale? Oh, maybe one in a thousand. Not worth it, you say? What does it cost you for a thousand cards? And what do you make on an average sale? If you've got the idea, start passing out those cards!

# Secret 3:
# Cultivate the Referral Farm

I've said this once, I'm going to say it again now, and I'll probably repeat it later: Referrals are the key to success in selling. Early in a sales career, of course, you're not going to have a lot of referral business coming in. That means many, many hours and days of coldcalling non-referred prospects. As time goes by, the referrals will build and you'll be able to rely on them more and more. The problem is, many salespeople don't last that long. It's tough paying the dues to build the base of satisfied customers who will become the source of referral business down the road. Once you're there, it's great. Getting there is murder. But like everything else in selling, your referral business will happen, and happen sooner, if you plan your work and work your plan for cultivating the referral farm. Here are some points for building that referral business.

## (1) Service, Follow-up, Service, Follow-up

Salespeople often make a critical error in their perception of the selling process. They work hard to identify a prospect, get the appointment, make the presentation, and close the sale. With the close, they get paid, they achieve satisfaction, and the process ends, or so they think. Their error is in failing to understand that the consummation of the sale is just the *beginning* of the process of achieving satisfaction for the customer. The lustful salesperson achieves his or her satisfaction and moves on to the next target, failing to build customer satisfaction and relationships which will lead to repeat business and referrals. By contrast, the professional salesperson understands the long-term payoff of cultivating the referral farm, and so makes the extra effort to enhance customer satisfaction *after* the close. That means repeated service and follow-up to demonstrate sincere customer interest and concern. It's an investment that pays attractive dividends. Sure, telling your prospect about all the features and benefits may get you a sale. But what you do after the sale, after you've been paid, will get you a referral.

It comes back to content/relationship all over again. People will recommend a product for its tangible, content aspects if, and only if, it also delivers satisfaction on the relational aspects. You won't recommend a great product if you dislike the people who represent it and the service they gave you. You will recommend a good product from people who were there after the sale.

# (2) Ask and Ye Shall Receive

One of the most fundamental tenets of salesmanship is that you've got to ask for the order. It's called closing and is the subject of the last chapter of this book. The importance of asking for the order isn't just restricted to your sales presentation, however. It's also the key to generating referral prospects. But if you don't ask, you probably won't get.

Generally, you'll ask for referrals from current satisfied customers. However, don't overlook potential referrals from all those persons with whom you've dealt in the past, perhaps even in seemingly unrelated fields. Here's a personal example to illustrate what I'm talking about. I established The Kimball Organization because I believed I had the experience and skills to develop and conduct sales and management training programs which would pay off in effectiveness and sales. On numerous occasions during the struggling fledgling days, I presented ideas and proposals to management. Initially, they expressed interest. Then, predictably, they'd ask me to identify companies for whom I'd done similar programs. As positively as possible, I'd have to tell them that they were going to be the first. You know what happened then. It was like looking for a job when everyone wants experience, but you can't get a job without experience and you can't get experience without a job. Catch 22.

The turning point in my business came when I presented a proposal in Birmingham to a company managed by Luke, someone I'd regularly worked with over a 12-year period when we were employed by the same or related companies. As in my prior proposals, all I could do was tell Luke and his managers that I believed I could develop good programs that would benefit their employees and their company. What was different this time was that Luke had considerable experience working with me. No, I'd never developed and conducted sales and management training programs for him. But he knew I would be committed to doing my best and doing what I said I'd do when I said I'd do it. I'm sure that was the deciding factor in me getting an opportunity to work with them.

If you've demonstrated your professionalism or helped someone enjoy the benefits of your product or service, that person will probably be more than happy to provide you with leads and referrals. Just be sure you've handled all the details of service and follow-up. Then, when you've delivered on everything you said you'd do and more, and the customer is expressing satisfaction, ask for a referral. If they appear amenable but can't think of anyone right off, isolate people for them to recall: "You mentioned you were president of your homeowner's association. Might this be a good investment for some of your members?" or "You said you were in a bowling league Wednesday nights. Do you think some of those folks would be interested in hearing about opportunities like this?"

Naturally, you don't want to be pushy or put your customer on the spot when asking for referrals. If you can, do so in an informal or relaxed atmosphere. Be alert. If the customer indicates satisfaction, that's your cue to ask for a referral. Seize the moment! Ask and ye shall receive.

Here's a personal example to illustrate my point. In the program developed for Luke's company, our first activity was a two-day retreat for him and his managers. During the day, we conducted sessions to help managers develop their management skills and set goals. Late afternoon and evening was set aside for rest and relaxation. Some of the participants went swimming, others did a little fishing, and a few gathered together on the porch to have a couple of cold ones and tell war stories. Luke and I, being dedicated runners, headed out to do several brisk miles around the north Alabama countryside. We got back about an hour later, physically tired but mentally invigorated. If you're a runner, you know what I mean. There we sat on the porch, making small talk, nothing heavy. Eventually, the conversation turned to the session we'd conducted that day, and I asked Luke what he thought of the program so far. He said he was real pleased and that several of his managers had told him it was the best they'd ever been to. Apparently, some of the most favorable comments had come from people who had initially expressed a lack of enthusiasm about attending. He concluded by saying that he could already see a beneficial impact on his people. Naturally, I was pleased. Then suddenly the light went on in my head and I said to myself, "Hey, Kimball, your customer is expressing satisfaction. That's a cue to ask for a referral. Act on it!" So, after saying something about being glad to hear he felt things were going well, I turned to him and said, "Luke, can you think of anyone else who might be able to benefit from a program like this?" He thought for a moment and said, "You might want to talk to Bill in Montgomery."

Needless to say, first thing Monday morning I was on the phone to Bill. I introduced myself and said that Luke had suggested I give him a call. I stated briefly that I was conducting some management and sales training activities in Birmingham, and that I believed he might be interested in hearing about what I could do for him in Montgomery. I then asked whether ten o'clock the next morning would be a convenient time for us to get together. Bill agreed, and bright and early the next morning I was headed down Interstate 85. I arrived about a quarter before ten, and Bill's secretary invited me to have a seat and a cup of coffee, saying that Bill would be with me just as soon as he got off the phone.

Guess who Bill was talking to on the phone? Right! Luke! And does it come as any surprise that in a follow-up meeting two days later with Bill and his top management, we ironed out all the specifics of programs for their 200 employees. Less than a week after conducting the first training activity for The Kimball Organization, I closed the sale for a second major program.

I don't tell you this to make me sound like some kind of big-time dealmaker, because that I am not. I cite it only as an example of the power of asking for a referral—after you've done your very best to help your customer enjoy all the benefits of your product or service, and that customer expresses satisfaction for a job well done. Do note that asking for a referral is *not* a request for someone to do you a favor. It *is* giving your customer the opportunity to help someone else enjoy the benefits you've delivered to them. So, when a customer tells you that you've done a good job, there's no reason to be shy. Ask for a referral. Ask and ye shall receive.

# (3) Get Some Birddawgs

When you're beatin' them bushes huntin' for quail, don't go it alone. Get you some birddawgs. If you're not a fan of the University of Georgia or the Cleveland Browns, you probably call them birddogs. This is sort of a variation on ask and ye shall receive. Earlier, I mentioned having the service department birddawg for you. That's one opportunity. Other, potentially even more lucrative opportunities, are your current satisfied customers. Sell them, give them some of your cards, and tell them that for every person they send to you who buys, they receive a birddawg fee.

Let's say you sell real estate. Why not have everyone from Betty's Beauty Barn to the local hardware store birddawging for you? Just have a little sign printed for them to display: "Interested in selling your home? See me." or "Interested in the best buy on the home of your dreams? See me." When a prospect inquires, the birddawg gives them one of your cards, with their name written on it. If the prospect buys, you pay the birddawg.

Generally, birddawging works best on products or services sold to individuals or families. Birddawging might be inappropriate, resented, or downright unethical in business-to-business transactions. Most companies frown upon, and have very strict prohibitions against, their employees accepting gratuities or kickbacks from suppliers. In such a situation, these business professionals generally would appreciate at least a thank-you note if they've provided a referral. Even more, they would appreciate a total commitment on your part to see that they and the referred prospect receive impeccable service, follow-up, and attention to detail. Should you feel compelled to do more, tell them you've sent a contribution to their favorite charity in their name.

# (4) Take a Ride on the Cycle

I don't mean the one with two or three wheels you ride around the neighborhood. I mean the regular repurchase cycle of your product. Some items follow a fairly regular repurchase pattern—maybe a year, maybe two, maybe five or more. The customer gets a new one and really enjoys it for a while. Then, it begins to wear a little and wear a little on him or her. The customer lusts for the new and improved model a buddy at the plant just got. It's time to step up. All the senses crave the smell of something new. It's hard to say what causes it, but I've always believed that a major factor is the approach of the final payment. Let's

face it, Americans love living on the edge of financial peril. It's unpatri-
otic not to worry about monthly payments. Remember when you looked
at your payment book and realized that in only six more months the car
would be yours? No more car payments! Wonderful thought. Remember
all those things you planned to do with that extra money you were
going to have every month? So what happened? Chances are you didn't
even make it to the last payment. If you did, I'll bet you couldn't stand
it any longer after one or two months. You began getting the itch to buy.
And when the itch starts, it's like falling in love. Initially, you're not
fully aware of what's happening to you. Then you deny it and fight it for
a while. Finally, it overwhelms you. You're a hot prospect, ready to buy.

If what you sell has a regular repurchase cycle, you need to get on the
cycle and contact customers when they're ready to buy. Naturally, I trust
you've been keeping in touch with these people all along, with thank-
you notes, cards, service, and follow-up. Then, when it looks like they're
about ready to get on the cycle again, give them a call, perhaps, as in
the next point, to upgrade them to whatever is bigger and better, smaller
and better, new and improved, the latest advancement, state-of-the-art.

# (5) Move Them Up

As just noted, when the repurchase cycle bug bites someone, it's a perfect time for you to point out all the features and benefits of the latest
technology and innovations of the item that is the next step up. Many
buyers, though, don't get the bug on any regular calendar cycle. As long
as what they have is on the cutting edge, they're happy. But let some
new breakthrough come along, be it six months or five years down the
road, and they're ready to buy again. Remember, this doesn't apply to
everyone, just the innovators and early adopters, those who are among
the first to latch on to the latest technological or design improvement.

Let's say you're a salesperson specializing in television sets. Only days
after high-definition television hits the market, you make two sales.
One is to a couple in their late fifties who have bought a new set every
eight to ten years for the last 35 years. Looks like an eight-to-ten-year
repurchase cycle, at which time they want to buy whatever is then at
the top of the line. Make a note—better write it down or you might forget—to give them a call in seven and a half years. By contrast, your
other sale is to a young professional couple in their late twenties, who
already own a remote-control, 150-channel-capability, 27-inch console
with all the goodies, which they purchased a scant two years ago. Kind

of short for a regular repurchase cycle? Looks as though these people want the latest technological improvement, irregardless of time. Now, let me ask you this: Three years later, when direct cable digital reception comes on line, providing a quantum leap in reception quality, who ya gonna call? Of course! The young couple! Even if it's only been three years, if they were among the first to step up to the latest advance in design then, it's likely they'll be among the first now. If you sold them the technological breakthrough three years ago, it's unthinkable to imagine that some other salesperson will sell them this time. Just don't assume they'll come to see you on their own. Give them a call.

And what about the older couple? Any point in calling them, too? Sure, why not? It's a good opportunity to maintain personal contact with them. You might also want to ask if they know of anyone else who's looking for a good value in a new television. Remind them of your birddawg program. This sure beats standing around the showroom, waiting for the next walk-in.

## (6) Comb the Desert

By now, I'm sure you appreciate the need to maintain contact with your customers. It's fundamental to building repeat business and referrals, which are, after all, the foundation of your success. Occasionally, however, one of your salespeople may retire or move on. Fairly often, someone goes to work for three or four months, stumbles across three or four sales, and then elects to seek employment with the government or a regulated utility where he or she can continue to sit on their butt all day, but now get paid for it. What about the deserted customers of these former salespeople? Who's going to take care of them now? Naturally, you are. Comb the desert and rescue those deserted customers. Make them *your* customers.

# Secret 4: Get the Appointment

So far, we've covered prospecting, an organized system for identifying qualified buyers who can benefit from your product or service. The next step is getting an appointment with that prospect to make your presentation in person. Generally, the request for an appointment is made through a telephone call. Remember this:

# The purpose of the telephone call is to get the appointment.

Let's repeat: The purpose of the telephone call is to get the appointment. Nothing more.

This is easier said than done. Before agreeing to an appointment, the prospect may ask about numerous details concerning your offering and, in an effort to convince them to grant you an audience, you roll right into your presentation/demonstration over the phone. This is an easy trap to fall into. The problem is, when the phone call requesting an appointment evolves into a presentation, you have virtually assured yourself of *not* getting the appointment and thus not getting the sale.

Obviously, I'm talking about selling situations in which your objective is to meet qualified buyers in person. If you're currently employed making 50¢ an hour over minimum wage doing telephone sales, this segment will not apply to you until you get a real job.

In the next chapter, I'll discuss essentials of an effective presentation/demonstration. At this point, suffice it to say, your presentation/demonstration is the vehicle by which you actively involve your prospect in discovering the benefits of your product or service. That means stimulating *all* their senses. They see it, they hear it, they smell, touch, and taste it. But what happens when you conduct your presentation sequence over the phone? You lose four of the five senses.

Another disadvantage of selling over the phone: there's no personal contact. Remember the importance of the relational dimension of communication? How can you develop trust and rapport across a telephone line? You simply can't. Relationships require face-to-face, eye-to-eye contact.

In the final chapter of this book, I go into closing the sale. Certainly no presentation is complete unless you ask for the order. But how do you know when it's time to close? Basically, you at least go for a trial close or a little-decision close any time the customer indicates agreement. The problem is, most such closing cues are nonverbal in nature, so over the phone you miss them. You also miss all the other behavioral cues which enable you to guide your presentation/demonstration sequence toward building agreement. One more time, then, so you don't forget:

# The sole purpose of the phone call is to get the appointment.

Here are a few points to keep in mind when you're preparing to get on the phone to make those appointments:

# (1) Think in Terms of Activity, Not Results

This sounds backwards, doesn't it? After all, you get paid for results, not methods and techniques. Thinking in terms of activity, though, can be useful in putting prospecting into perspective. Let's face it: You're going to get a lot more refusals than appointments. In most circumstances, but no more than 95 percent of the time, prospects can be rude, insulting, or may even hang up without saying goodbye and wishing you a nice day. Consider cars. What do you think the odds are that a telephone call will lead to a customer taking a test drive and buying a car? Would you say one in a hundred? How about one in two hundred? And what do you make in commission off that sale? A few hundred dollars? Do you seriously think it's worth it to be insulted, sworn at, rejected, and hung up on 199 times to find the needle in the haystack who will buy? The results don't seem worthwhile.

On the other hand, what would you say if I made you this offer: I want you to do some cold-call prospecting for me and I'll pay you one dollar for every call you complete, regardless of the result. They buy, they hang up, they tell you off—it makes no difference. You get one dollar a call. Interested? Given that the vast preponderance of those called will probably terminate the call in 20 seconds or less, I estimate you could knock out 50 or 60 calls an hour. Of course you're interested!

So, what's the difference between those two scenarios—between being rejected 199 times to make one sale and being paid a dollar every time you place a call? The fact is, there is no difference. Over the long haul, you earn a dollar for each call. Sure, you may go 500 calls in a row without a hit. On the other hand, you may get two live ones on consecutive days. It all evens out. Calculate your own ratios. Figure the average commission you earn for each appointment you get, and divide that by the number of calls it takes to get one appointment. By focusing on activity rather than results, you may find it worthwhile to get on the phone for an hour during a slow time of day instead of sitting around with your fellow salespeople drinking coffee, talking about how lousy business is, while you wait for the next customer to come in.

# (2) Start with the Receptionist

You may already know who the decision makers are, how they pronounce and spell their names, what their exact titles are, and their mailing addresses, including zip code. If so, fine. Ask to talk to those people. If, on the other hand, you're one iota less than 100 percent certain about anything, ask the receptionist and get everything straight first. Also, with receptionists, secretaries, assistants, janitors, parking lot attendants, security personnel, or *any* other support staff people at your customer's place of business: Be nice to them. Smile, be courteous, and get to know their names. Treat them no differently than you would the big boss you're calling on for a million dollar sale. There are a few reasons for this. First of all, everyone deserves respect and consideration. If you have to prove how important you are by acting pompous or rude to those you deem inferior, your prospects for a successful sales career are dim at best. And second, less philosophical and more pragmatic, those "underlings" can make or break you, and don't you ever forget it. A secretary who likes you can find a way to squeeze you in for a 15-minute appointment. Just try and get past one who doesn't care for you.

# (3) The Secretary Is the Key

You may think that all secretaries do is type, answer phones, and make coffee. If so, you are not a successful executive. *All* successful executives understand that there is a one-to-one relationship between their own success and the competence of their secretary. And one of the most important secretarial roles is that of the *gatekeeper*: Be sure the boss meets with those people he or she ought to see; screen out and eliminate those of no value; and delegate to a lower-level person or department those determined to have some value, though insufficient to deserve the personal attention of the boss. If you're blocked out completely, the game is over. And it's not much better to get shuffled off to a staff person or the personnel department. What you must do, then, is to convince the secretary to put you through to the decision maker for the opportunity to state your reason for asking for an appointment.

Occasionally, a secretary may schedule an appointment for you without having to talk to the decision maker first. This happens very rarely. Generally, you're going to have to get past the secretary by a convincing argument that you have something of interest and importance to the boss and/or the company, and second, that it's necessary to speak to the boss briefly to determine whether an appointment would be desirable. Remember what we said before: Your objective at this stage is only to get the appointment. Especially with the secretary, say little else other than to underscore the need for an appointment. Like this:

> Secretary: "Mrs. Johnson's office."
>
> You: "Hi. This is Fred Frumpp. Is she in, please?"
>
> Secretary: "Just a moment and I'll check." (The secretary knows good and well she's in. This is just the basic screening routine.) "Who are you with, Mr. Frumpp?"

At this point, if you have a referral from someone familiar to the prospect, use it here. It should get you through.

> You: "I'm with Consolidated Particleboard. Bob Benson suggested that I give her a call."

If you don't have a referral, or if you still haven't gotten through, you know what's coming next:

> Secretary: "What does this concern, please?"

On one particularly frustrating day, I answered that with "His wife's gambling debts." Believe it or not, I got through to the decision maker and confirmed the appointment. Better something like:

> You: "We've been doing some studies on marketing and distribution. I have some ideas I believe she'd be interested in hearing about. Is she in, please?"

If the secretary continues to press for more details or suggests exiling you to a subordinate, hold firm, offer no more information, and again request to be put through:

> You: "I believe Mrs. Johnson would wish to discuss this personally, and she'll know in just a few minutes if it's something she'd wish to consider. Could I talk with her, please?"

It may be difficult, but be nice and be courteous, even though you may feel like saying, "Hey, just stop screening me and put me through!"

If, after all this, the prospect is out or "away from her desk," the secretary may go through the formality of asking for your number for a call-back. It's been my experience—and it's probably yours, too—that prospects do not return your calls, but there is no harm in leaving your number. Just do so with a comment like, "She'll be able to reach me at this number until 2:00 P.M. If she can't call me by then, when would be a convenient time for me to call back?" That way, you've been given implied consent to phone back when your call isn't returned. This is a good time to ask the secretary's name, too.

# (4) Close for the Appointment in 45 Seconds or Less

When you get the prospect on the line, identify yourself, your company, the name of a referrer, and a very brief statement of your credentials, expertise, and experience. Then, say why you're calling, citing a very general benefit and requesting an appointment. Be prepared for what will probably happen next: The prospect will ask you to explain a little more before agreeing to a meeting. Just remember: The more you say at this point, the less likely you are to ever get that appointment. Simply state something along the lines of "I wish I could explain all of this over the phone, but. . .," and then give them a rationale as to why they really need to see you in person. A suggestion: Before you call, be prepared with a few reasons why it would be beneficial for them to meet with you.

There's one more thing about getting the appointment. Often, your prospect may indicate some interest, but will suggest you see someone at a lower level in the organization. Many an over-anxious salesperson has grasped at such an opportunity as a way to get a foot in the door; but my experience has been that you're spinning your wheels talking to anyone other than the decision maker with budgetary responsibility.

Again, *before* you call, think of valid reasons why the decision maker should be present, perhaps with the lower-level people also attending. If the prospect balks, ask if the lower-level person has the latitude to make a buying decision if favorably impressed with your proposal. If the answer is yes, you may wish to go ahead. If the answer is no, it enables you to show this as the reason why the prospect should meet with you in person, so you can clarify any important points.

Should the prospect indicate that the lower-level person does not have buying authority, but that the two of them will meet later to discuss your proposal, you can forget it. Experienced salespeople who have burned up expense accounts and wasted entire days with non-decision makers know what I mean. The rest of you won't take my word for it and will try it a few times anyway. You'll learn.

# Secret 5: Do Some Pre-Approach Preparation

This seems so fundamental you'd think every salesperson would do it, but they don't. When you hang up the phone, appointment in hand, it's time to begin working on the little extras that can make the sales call a winner.

Every customer is different. Each buys differently and for different reasons. That means you need to customize your presentation/demonstration for every customer and every situation. The performance that got four stars in Peoria may bomb in Green Bay.

As a Kimball-trained sales professional, you're already an expert on your product, customer, competition, and industry. Now, though, it's time to procure even more detailed information which can give you that little edge—the difference between a good presentation and a good presentation which results in a sale. For starters, find out all you can about the personality, interests, and buying style of the decision maker. An analytic gets a different presentation than an expressive. Select industry trends and issues most relevant to this particular firm. Ask around. Inquire about any relevant experiences of your boss or peers. If someone gave you a referral, either directly or through a swapping party, bird-dawg, or other secondary source, check with them. And don't forget the prospect's secretary, who now knows you by phone, is your ally, and is looking forward to meeting you in person.

Some benefits are germane to many or all companies. Use them in your presentation, of course. Additionally, cite at least one issue, problem, or opportunity which is of particular concern to this prospect and company. If you can't think of any, you need to do a little more home-work.

Don't get so focused on the economic decision maker that you ignore other people in the organization who are buying influences. Like those who will be using it and will have to live with it. Don't sell the boss on a word processing system and fail to get the secretaries and their supervisors on board. Don't sell a widget maker and install it on the factory floor without getting the operators and foremen fired up about what it can do and how it will make their work and life so much better. Those who use and are directly involved with your product or service will take it personally since it affects their daily routine. They can be very supportive and helpful if you bring them on board. They can be resentful, uncooperative, or even sabotage you if ignored.

Also, you'd better be familiar with the prospect's technical people and the technical evaluation criteria used to determine whether your offering meets specifications. Those technical people don't control the purse strings—they can't say yes—but if your proposal falls short in any of their criteria, they can say no and often do.

Many companies will not permit your salespeople to interact with their technical people. However, they may allow your technical people to do so. If that's the case, get your technical people involved early on, preferably before you develop your proposal.

Particularly if you're heading into unfamiliar and uncharted waters, get yourself a coach. Coaches can be found in your organization, the buyer's organization, or just about anywhere else. Their role is to act as a guide for the sale and to advise you in strategy for preparing your proposal and dealing with all the buying influences. In considering someone as a prospective coach, be sure that you have credibility and are trusted by that person. Additionally, the coach must have credibility within the buying organization and must want you to succeed. Approach this person with a request for advice and counsel. Try the three little words "I need help." Do *not* ask for a referral or for a good word on your behalf to the decision maker. Ask for a referral or a good word and you probably won't get it or coaching. Ask for advice and help instead. Then, you'll be more likely to get coaching and a referral.

Finally, do everything possible to pre-plan your call and the presentation/demonstration. Put yourself in the customer's shoes. What are their needs, problems, and opportunities you can address with features that can be translated to benefits? What are their likely objections and how do you plan to respond to those objections? No one likes objections and I know you'd rather not think of them. On the other hand, it's a safe bet you will get objections. It's better to think about them in advance and have an answer ready than to have one hit you between the eyes in the presentation. You'll stumble and mumble through an attempt to answer it, and then, two minutes later, think of the perfect response—unfortunately, two minutes too late to do you any good. In Chapter Seven, we'll go into objections in detail and see how to turn them from obstacles into opportunities.

Having thought through the situation, select your presentation materials and write out your plan for the call. Practice, practice, practice what you're going to say and do, and how your demonstration will enable the prospect to discover the truth and benefits for himself or herself. Write down points of agreement on which you will attempt to close the sale. And above all, set a specific goal for the call:

## What action and commitment is your objective?

It should be obvious that any salesperson must have a specific call objective. Otherwise, as Yogi says, if you don't know where you're going, you might wind up somewhere else. Along with your primary goal, set a secondary fallback position. For example: Your call objective is to get product distribution in your prospect's 500 stores nationwide. Your secondary fallback position is to test it in 100 stores in the Southwest, evaluate sales for 60 days, and then consider a national rollout.

# Summing Up

This chapter has focused on the Five Top Secrets of Prospecting and Preparation for the call. Let's review them:

- **Secret 1:** Qualification is the key. Sure, you want to get out and meet prospects face-to-face. Just be sure those prospects are qualified. Don't waste your time or the time of prospects who don't have the wherewithal to pay for all those benefits you're offering.

- **Secret 2:** Build a base of suspects. This is your extensive list of non-referred prospects from which you'll select targets for cold calls.

- **Secret 3:** Cultivate the referral farm. That's your strategy for building referrals and identifying prequalified prospects.

- **Secret 4:** Get the appointment. Convince qualified buyers to meet with you in person.

- **Secret 5:** Do your pre-approach preparation. Do your homework and get yourself organized and prepared for the call.

Looks like you're ready to roll. You determined who to call, got an appointment with the qualified decision maker, have set goals for the call, and are fully prepared. Now it's time to get into the appropriate attire and head out the door. The next stop is the presentation/demonstration.

**CHAPTER 5**

# A Sales Call Is a Performance

---

## The Six Top Secrets for Making Your Presentation a Winner

Finally, all your preparations are complete. You found a qualified prospect. You identified the decision maker and got an appointment. You've done all your homework; you know everything there is to know about everyone and everything. You've planned and thoroughly rehearsed your presentation/demonstration. Your materials and samples are prepared. It's time to make the sales call. It's show time!

Show time, you may ask? But this is a sales call, not a stage performance. Wrong! A sales call *is* a performance. It's a show! You're an actor. You're on stage. And the same principles that make for success on the stage or screen will make for success in your presentation. No, your objective is not *solely* to entertain, but your performance *must* excite and entertain the audience, your prospect.

In this chapter, we'll get into the Six Top Secrets for Making Your Presentation a Winner. The first secret is to be sure that all meeting room conditions and arrangements are right. That means checking out the room and your equipment in advance to avoid any unpleasant surprises.

The secrets of a successful performance include an effective opening to build rapport with your prospects. Then, a planned sequence of questions to identify buying motives, get them to talk, and help them discover the truth themselves. During the presentation, you must involve your prospects by creating images in their minds which visualize the benefits of your product or service. And finally, never lose sight of the objective of your presentation—closing the sale!

Well, you've arrived at the location of your meeting. You're there in plenty of time. You're fully prepared, though with a butterfly or two churning around in your stomach. You walk in the door. The curtain is about to rise. It's show time! You're confident of success, because you've remembered the Six Top Secrets of the Presentation/Demonstration.

# Secret 1:
# Clean Up Your Room

I have seen—I'll bet you have, too—numerous sales presentations and meetings that were unmitigated disasters. In a few of those cases, the presenter was either unprepared, lost his or her composure, or said or did something wrong. In most cases, though, the disaster stemmed from the room, the room arrangements, or the equipment. Wherever you make a presentation or hold a meeting, be it in a decision maker's office to one person or in an auditorium to an audience of a few hundred or more, don't take anything for granted. Allow sufficient time to check out and clean up your room, the equipment, and all the arrangements for the meeting. As Murphy reminds us, anything that *can* go wrong *will* go wrong, at the least opportune moment. But most of the things that can go wrong are preventable if you take steps in advance. Here are some points to remember about setting up the room and related arrangements. I'm sure that some, most, or all of these have happened at meetings or presentations you've attended. Just don't let any of them happen at meetings or presentations you conduct.

# (1) Check Out the Size of the Room and the Number and Arrangement of Seats

It should be obvious that you need a room of a size sufficient to accommodate all your attendees and that there be enough seats for everyone. It's unthinkable that any meeting be delayed while people go around to adjacent rooms trying to scrounge up chairs, but it happens.

If your meeting room is too small and guests feel like sardines, they're not going to feel comfortable. When people do not feel comfortable, their instinct is to escape from that environment. If their escape mechanism is activated, just what do you figure your chances are of gaining their attention and interest?

While a room that's too small is bad, a room that's too large isn't all that much better. In your presentation you need to establish interpersonal communication and dialogue. If you have four people in a room that will hold four hundred, their focus of attention will expand to fill all the empty space. That means away from you. So when you set up your meeting, determine how many people will be attending and procure a room of appropriate size. It should be just big enough, though never too small.

Another consideration for a meeting room is the arrangement of seats. Are you using a slide projector? If so, set up the seats so people can face you while you're speaking and also so they won't have to move or turn around when you show the slides. Also, don't forget to make an aisle to project through to the screen. How many times have you been to a presentation when someone's head got in the way of the projection? Don't let that happen to you.

The same considerations apply if you're using a flip chart or a VCR. Position the seats so your audience can see all the elements of your presentation by shifting their eyes or slightly turning their head. Also, make sure your visuals are big enough for everyone to see clearly. That's less of a problem with slides or an overhead projector, where you can fill up an entire screen. It may be a problem with a VCR. If so, set up your equipment with more than one TV monitor. A flip chart can also be hard for everyone to see. If the person in the last row can't read your figures, you have a problem. So use big, wide bar graphs to illustrate your points.

If you're using audiovisuals in your presentation, you also need to check out the lighting. No one can see a flip chart in a shadow. Have it positioned so that it's got enough light on it. An overhead projector generally presents no problems. It's bright enough that your audience can see the screen clearly with the lights left on; but if you want to turn the lights off, the projector will illuminate the room enough for people to be able to see you, each other, and take notes. A VCR will probably be no problem, and dimming the lights may enhance viewing while enabling the audience to see around them and take notes. If the lights can't be dimmed, leave them on if the audience needs to see or do anything other than watch the screen.

Slides are a different story. If the lights are on, people won't be able to see the slides. If the lights are off, they won't be able to see you, each other, or take notes. If that's no problem, fine. If it is, you'd better check the room in advance to be sure there's a dimming capability on the lights. Should there be no dimming capability, you have two ways to go—get a different room or revise your presentation accordingly.

A final consideration with the room is the view—or, hopefully, the lack of one. A room with a view may be ideal for a San Francisco apartment, but not for a meeting or presentation. The absolute worst situation is for you to attempt to make a presentation at a hotel meeting room which overlooks the swimming pool. Not much better is a room which affords any view of the outdoors, particularly if a line of thunderstorms is rolling in or if it's the day of the season's first snowfall. Close the drapes or change the room.

# (2) Check Out All other Potential Meeting Room Glitches

If Muzak is playing, get it turned off. Also, double-check in advance to be sure there will be no noise emanating from adjacent rooms or other surroundings. If you're making your presentation at a hotel or convention center, you might assume they wouldn't be operating jackhammers on the floor above at the scheduled time of your meeting. Or you might assume they would never book another meeting in the room next door, separated only by a moveable partition. In the days of my naive youth, I once opened a luncheon meeting at the stroke of twelve with "Ladies and gentlemen, I'd like to welcome you to..." when the sound of a piano chimed through the moveable partition and the meeting next door joined in the singing of the National Anthem. I paused to let them finish—what else could I do?—and started from scratch. I got through "Ladies and gentlemen, I'd like to..." when the group next door started on the Pledge of Allegiance. Again, I paused, lest anyone think me a leftist pinko commie. They finished, and I started my introduction a third time, fully expecting a chorus of "Amazing Grace" next. That didn't happen, but the respective meetings each turned into a shouting match in an attempt to be heard by our own attendees while simultaneously drowning out the speaker next door. Since that event, I now assume nothing and always verify in advance that the room will be quiet.

Often, you will wish to place posters, point-of-sale materials, or related items on the meeting room walls. That can present a problem. Don't expect to use stick pins. They can be difficult to push into cinder block, and they may not create a good impression stuck in the mahogany walls of your prospect's boardroom. Many companies, therefore, supply their salespeople with that silly-putty-type adhesive. If your company gives that to you, do yourself a favor and trash it now. It doesn't work. Well, maybe I shouldn't say that. It does work, sort of. You put up your posters with it about half an hour before the meeting begins. Everything's fine at the start. Then, about ten minutes into your presentation, the corner on one of the posters comes loose and kind of hangs over. A couple of minutes later, the corner on another poster goes. Then another. Pretty soon, the stress on the remaining upper corner on one of the posters is too much. It gives. The bottom corners immediately fail and it noisily flutters to the floor. By this time, you've totally lost your audience—they are organizing a lottery to make book on which poster will fall next.

My experience has been that if you want to hang posters or point-of-sale on the walls, go out and get yourself a roll of duct tape. Take a six-inch strip and make a loop with the sticky side out. Put a loop on each of the four corners of each poster. Duct tape will hold anything up, even heavy cardboard, and it won't damage the walls.

One last item on meeting room glitches: If you are having any kind of meal or beverage service, there is a 65 percent chance of a foul-up. The wrong food, the wrong time, the wrong room. The day before, and the day of your meeting, verify everything with catering. If your meeting starts at 8:00, make sure they understand you want the coffee and rolls to be there at 7:30. How often have you gone to a meeting, anticipating the coffee and rolls at 7:30, and at 7:45, still nothing. At that point, someone sends a gopher down to catering to find out what's going on. He gets back at 7:50 to report that they thought your meeting was at 9:00 and that you wanted coffee and rolls at 8:30, but that it's on the way. It gets to be 8:00, and they delay opening the meeting until the coffee and rolls arrive. By 8:15, nothing yet, and they decide we'd better get started. At 8:25, the coffee and rolls arrive at the back of the room. About half the attendees head back there to help themselves, mouthing words or communicating in sign language with their cohorts to ascertain what they want in their coffee and whether they'd prefer apricot, blueberry, or plain. Attention and meeting continuity is lost.

Same thing on breaks, dinner, lunch, happy hour, or hors d'oeuvres. Double check and verify every detail, and not just with the front office. Speak to those people who will do the actual serving.

# (3) Check Out the Equipment

Make sure your equipment works, and make sure you have spare bulbs. When the bulb blows on the overhead projector, it's no problem to call a five-minute stretch break while you change it. By contrast, you've got big trouble if you have to send someone over to the camera store in the mall to buy one.

I always carry a 100-ft. heavy-duty extension cord with me. And I used to think that was overkill until I recently had to use an overhead projector for a presentation in an auditorium. The only outlets were at the back of the room, 90 feet away. If I'm going to be using someone else's slide projector, I also carry my own 25-foot extension cord for the remote-control switch. Slide projectors have a long focal length, which means you have to set them up 20 to 25 feet back from the screen. Without an extension cord, the remote-control switch is about six feet long, which means you may not be able to stand in front of your audience to make your presentation.

Finally, if you're going to set up equipment or demonstration materials on your prospect's desk or on a nice piece of furniture, bring along a pad of some kind to place underneath it. You know how you feel when someone sets a beer can on your beautiful new coffee table. Prospects feel the same way about their office.

As you've read through all these points on meeting rooms, arrangements, and equipment, I'm sure you've thought that all of it is common sense and obvious. I agree that it's common sense. But apparently it's not obvious, since salespeople fail to finalize these details every day. That lessens the effectiveness of a meeting or a presentation, and that lessens the probability of a sale. Don't let it happen to you. Clean up your room!

# Secret 2:
# Set the Table with Your Opening

You've been in this situation: You're at a business or social function and across the room you spot someone you'd really like to meet. But you freeze. You know that once a conversation gets underway between the two of you, everything will go smoothly and you'll glide through your presentation toward the objective of the call, so to speak. The problem is getting started. You need a good opening line. In a social situation, people often hit you with something like "Are you from here?" or "Haven't I seen you someplace before?" Thankfully, "What's your sign?" appears to have disappeared since the 1980s. Few if any of these openers, though, do much in gaining the attention and interest of the potential client. The same thing is true of the opening lines of many salespeople. And if your opening is a bomb, just what chance do you think there is that your presentation will be a winner?

The professional salesperson sets objectives and plans the opening the same way he or she sets objectives and plans the presentation itself. You set the table with the opening. You serve the meal with the presentation. The filet mignon and wine of the presentation won't do you much good if you neglected to lay out the silverware and glasses in the opening.

The first thing you have to do in the opening is to establish rapport, find common ground, and get on the same wavelength as your prospect. Go back to the scenario of seeing that appealing someone across the room at a social function. You know better than to just walk up to that person with a cheap opening line. If you have any cool at all, you might first just walk toward them, smile, say "Hi," and keep walking. Since you're not confronting or imposing, the person is comfortable and chances are good he or she will say "Hi" and smile back. Maybe ten minutes later you spot your prospect at the appetizer table and casually saunter over there yourself, make eye contact, and say something like, "These shrimp are great." If the other person comments about the food, you may begin to engage in conversation then and there. If not, perhaps another 20 minutes later you meet again and, now that you're no longer a total stranger, you can make another casual comment, ranging from "Do you work in the PR Department?" to "Did you see that Rolls-Royce on fire in the parking lot?" By this point, if you had any chance of getting the appointment, you've begun your presentation. If not, you've moved on to the next prospect.

This chapter is not going to degenerate into tactics for being a social success at the company cocktail party. I cite this example solely to point out what anyone past the eighth grade should know: In the opening, you take it easy and go slow. Let the other person see you, look you over, and get comfortable before you begin to establish a dialogue.

The same in selling. If you're employed in a retail showroom, **do not** immediately walk up to customers, hit them with "May I help you?" and stand there. Such an approach virtually guarantees a "No, thank you, we're just looking." If your next step is to follow them around as they look, you'll likely drive them out of the store in 60 seconds or less.

Instead, smile, say "Hi," and introduce yourself. If they want to give you their name at that point, great. Just be sure and remember it. You'll look pretty stupid if you have to ask for it again later. Then, welcome them to your place of business and ask a helpful, caring question such as, "Is there anything in particular you're looking for today?" If there is, show it to them. If not, invite them to look around and then permit them to walk away from you. Yes! Let them go! Let them move around at their own pace, by themselves. Naturally, you don't ignore them. Keep them in sight but don't stare. When—and if—they settle around one particular item for a minute or so, casually walk over and ask an opening involvement question like "Will you be using this in your living room?" By this time, you're familiar to them, and, if they've been looking at something for at least a minute, they've apparently found something they're interested in. Now begin presenting.

The scenario is different if you're calling on a prospect at his or her place of business, but the same principles apply. If you've never met before, take a few moments for small talk. Be prepared with some comments about the company, the place of business, or something favorable you've heard about that person. Maybe tell a few war stories about the person who gave you a referral, or find an interest or hobby in which you can establish common ground.

If you do know each other, double-check to be sure there are no loose ends or details that require your attention or follow-up, such as no problems with shipping, billing, or credits. Get the prospect away from distractions, be they secretaries, co-workers, customers, or phone calls. You can't start your presentation until you have that person's undivided attention.

It's critical that you control the duration of the opening. Too short and the table isn't set. Too long and you're wasting their time. The opening takes longer sitting on a front porch with an amiable than it does in a purchasing department office with an analytic. Be alert. When you perceive that you've established rapport and are communicating on the customer's wavelength, that's your cue to move out of the opening and into the presentation. That's when you make your "opening statement."

The opening statement is what you say to shift out of the small talk and into the business at hand. As such, it must galvanize the prospect's attention and interest and create a desire to hear more.

Part of your pre-approach preparation should be to prepare one or more opening statements for your presentation. Avoid you-focused, product-focused statements like "I'd like to show you. . ." or "Our company is introducing a new. . . ." The opening statement should be a customer-focused benefit statement such as "My reason for calling on you today is that I have an idea which I believe can save you as much as 10 percent on production costs." Or ". . .could bring an additional 500 customers a month in your store." Generally, the opening statement should address and build upon those benefits you cited when calling the prospect to request an appointment. Additionally, it must convince the prospect that he or she wants and needs to hear your presentation. It should address a problem or opportunity, offer a benefit that hits a hot button, and begin your presentation with a bang.

# Secret 3:
# Use Questions to Be Effective

Your opening statement moves you out of the opening phase of the call and into the presentation itself. And this is the stage where many salespeople—successful to this point of the call—begin to lose the game. That's because they think that what they do in a presentation is to present. They go through the spiel, do the dog-and-pony show, and ask for the order. Yes, that's part of the process, of course. But it's the lesser, not the predominant part of the process. That's because when a professional salesperson makes a presentation, he or she will listen more than speak. In a presentation, you should listen—with the prospect speaking—at least 55 percent of the time. If you're doing more than 45 percent of the talking, it's time to pull back on the reins, talk less, and listen more. You just aren't going to persuade the prospect with your brilliant oratory. On the contrary, you persuade the prospect by getting him or her to talk. And you do that through the skillful use of questions in the sales interview. Yes, questions rather than statements. And even though it's called a "presentation," presenting is only part of it. To be effective, a presentation is really an *interview,* involving a two-way dialogue between you and your prospect.

Let's look at specific objectives and purposes of questions in the sales interview:

(1) Questions enable you to tune into the prospect and their thinking, to establish a comfortable dialogue and rapport.

(2) Questions help you qualify prospects and identify their needs, buying motives, and hot button.

(3) Questions give the prospect a greater sense of participation. They get prospects involved and help them discover and identify problems without being put on the defensive.

(4) Questions help you take control of the interview by building agreement and moving toward the close by getting the prospect to confirm an understanding of benefits and their importance. Remember that when you talk about a benefit, your prospect may not be convinced. But when the prospect confirms it, that's a closing cue.

The average salesperson plans the presentation. The professional salesperson also plans sequences of questions which will move the interview toward a close. Let's walk through a typical sequence to demonstrate how effective questioning can help attain the objectives of the call.

**Start with high-structured questions to get information and obtain specific facts.**   Although you want to begin with questions that are easy to answer, don't ever ask a question that can be answered "Yes" or "No." Begin with directive questions such as "What brand are you using now?"; "How long have you had it?"; "About how many units do you produce each year?"

**Shift to low-structured questions to get a general idea of the prospect's feelings and attitudes.**   You might ask an evaluative question such as "Are you entirely satisfied with that unit and the service support you're getting?" to initiate a sequence which makes the prospect think and helps you discover a possible dissatisfaction and buying motive.

Let's say the response to the last question was along the line of, "Well, yes, I'd say we're satisfied." What does that mean? Are they satisfied or aren't they? Maybe yes, maybe no. And maybe they really aren't all that satisfied but haven't thought about it that much. In any case, the prospect is highly unlikely to come right out and admit he or she is not satisfied but hasn't done anything about it. That would make your prospect look bad.

**Follow up with more high-structured directive questions.**   These are questions like "What do you like most about the XWD–16 you're using now? and "What would you like to see modified or improved in that unit?" Similarly, do the "like most" and "like to see modified or improved" sequence for service support.

Think about what those questions have done for you. "Like most" has identified benefits important to the prospect, benefits you need to address when you present. "Like to see modified or improved" has identified benefits important to the prospect but currently unfulfilled. That means you've uncovered a possible dissatisfaction or hot button on which to focus. And the prospect, who started off saying, "Well, yes, I'd say we're satisfied" has begun to consider the possibility that the company is not all that satisfied after all. Through questions, though, you've let the prospect discover it and say it without getting defensive. By contrast, if you'd hit him or her between the eyes with all the shortcomings of the present product and service support, you'd have said a potential customer was wrong, with bad business judgment. And as we all know, customers are never wrong.

**Get the prospect to elaborate on all those "like to see modified or improved" responses.**    In other words, let your prospect convince herself or himself of the present dissatisfaction level. Then that prospect becomes receptive to a solution to the problem he or she wasn't even consciously aware of only minutes before. Let's say the response to your question about the product was "I'd like to see them improve the feeder mechanism on the XWD–16." First ask some directive questions to begin the talk about the specific kinds of problems:

> You: "What experiences are you having with the feeder mechanism?"
>
> Customer: "Well, it seems to jam more often than it should."
>
> You: "How often is it doing that?"
>
> Customer: "Oh, three or four times a week. And it always seems to happen in the middle of a run."

When you get your prospects started with directive questions, they're selling themselves on things that should be modified or improved. You sure don't want the talk to stop now, so help through low-structured elaboration questions to get your prospect to provide even further details:

> You: "How has that affected your production schedules and operating efficiency?"
>
> Customer: "I guess it's caused us a few problems."

Here again, through the use of a question rather than a statement, the salesperson has the prospect agreeing that the present product has problems. Contrast that to the reaction you could expect from you stating, "And every time it jams, your production schedules and operating efficiency are adversely affected." The *question* enables the prospect to discover needs and problems and talk about them. The *statement* is accusatory and invites a defense rather than receptivity.

When the professional salesperson elicits a response such as "I guess it's caused us a few problems," he or she will encourage the prospect to elaborate further:

> You: "What sort of things have happened?"

Customer:    "Well, last week, for instance. It jammed and went down for an hour."

You:    "Really?" The "Really?" or a "Hmm. . ." or even a nod of the head isn't actually a question but more of a regulator which indicates to the prospect that he or she should continue speaking.

Customer:    "Yeah, it took us half a day to get back on schedule."

And so forth and so forth.

There's a variation to this approach when you're already aware of a problem your prospect is having and you directly employ a high-structured question which points out a competitive disadvantage. Remember always to be careful when knocking the competition. You may do so, however, by framing the statement in the form of a question: "Many of our customers formerly had an XWD–16, and they told us it tended to have a problem with jamming. Has that been your experience?" You would not use this direct approach unless you were confident of getting an affirmative response. If, however, the prospect responded with "No, we haven't had any problems at all," the use of a question enables you to drop the point and move on.

The judicious use of questions has enabled you to identify those benefits which are important to your prospect, and determined which benefits they're satisfied with or not.

**Complete the sequence with open-ended questions such as "Can you think of anything else which might be important to you in considering such an item?" or closed-ended questions like "How helpful would it be to have service support available on 30 minutes notice, 24 hours a day, 7 days a week?"** Now, and only now that you have an understanding of the prospect's needs and the benefits that will satisfy those needs, do you begin to move toward the presentation itself. It's so simple, isn't it? Why would you want to waste your time, or your prospect's time, talking about benefits that are of no importance to that prospect? And yet, that's what salespeople do every day by marching right into their presentation without first asking questions to identify those needs and help the prospect uncover important benefits they're not getting now.

**Tie it all together with a reflective question, a high-structured summary statement which confirms understanding, gets a yes, and makes a prospect tell you to go ahead with your presentation.** "So, from what you're telling me, if you could have a machine as compact and durable as the XWD–16, with a feeder that could reduce your lost downtime from jamming by as much as 50 percent, at no increase in total cost, that would help your company, wouldn't it?" Since you've assumed control of the sales interview with your questions, the response, of course, is "Yes." You've not only begun your presentation, you've already begun to close.

# Secret 4:
# Create Images of Success for Your Prospect

Think back for a moment to some of those points on communication that were covered in Chapter Three. We discussed how people use logic to justify decisions that may be primarily affected by emotions and feelings. Selling with just facts and logic is like a race car trying to win the Indianapolis 500 without spark plugs. Emotions and feelings are what ignite the desire to buy. And to build those emotions and feelings, you must go beyond the facts and content of your presentation. You must create vivid images in the mind of your prospect. Here are three points to help you create those images of success.

## (1) Start with Your Personal Image

Part of this is effective nonverbal communication and impression formation, as we've discussed, including positive eye contact with your audience. Equally important, though, is the image of professionalism that your presentation must create. Remember: It's show time! Your presentation is a performance, designed to interest, entertain, and persuade. To be successful, it must be completely and perfectly rehearsed. Note that I said rehearsed, not canned. Some salespeople are under the mistaken impression that preparation means word-for-word memorization. There are two reasons why this isn't true. First of all, reciting something word for word just doesn't sound spontaneous and natural. Come across as reading to your audience and you're well on your way to losing them.

Secondly, when you've memorized a canned presentation, you have no flexibility. Sales presentations are not a stage play where the other party provides you a predictable, scripted response. Customers have been known to interrupt, to raise unanticipated questions and objections, and to take the conversation in a different direction. Your image as a sales professional is not determined by your ability to recite canned responses to predictable questions. It *is* determined by your ability to effectively handle points and issues that come up as you guide the presentation toward building agreement and negotiating a close. Not memorizing, but thoroughly understanding everything there is to know about your product, customer, competition, and industry. And utilizing presentation materials which cue you and guide you through the presentation.

Plan and prepare as you will, the unexpected will come up. And you're going to make mistakes. Let's face it, your image of competence and professionalism won't be as good the first time you make a presentation as it should be the tenth time. Don't worry about that. Think of it as a learning experience and an opportunity to improve your sense of humor. Just remember that the unexpected happens only once. And mistakes need not be repeated. That's why a sales professional immediately and carefully critiques every call. Think about how you could have better handled the unexpected and how not to make the same mistake in the future. Play out in your mind how you would handle such a situation in the future and what pre-approved preparation is necessary to prevent a recurrence of a mistake. Don't kick yourself for what happened in the past, but become prepared for the future. That's the beginning of confidence and an effective personal image.

# (2) Build High-Quality Visuals into Your Presentation

There are three reasons for these visuals. One, they enhance the image of presentation itself. Consider the impression of full-color, professionally lettered visuals compared to a black-and-white typed page. Which one conveys the image *you* wish to present? And today you can produce these yourself on many personal computers.

A second reason to utilize visuals in your presentation is that they get more of the prospects' senses involved. Sure, you want them to hear what you have to say. But a visual gives them a more active part to play in the presentation, looking at and touching something.

Finally, visuals are a device to help cue you through the presentation. In outline form, they guide you through the points you wish to cover. Just don't read them word for word. For instance, a visual might read:

Category                        +41%
Our Brand                       +85%
The Opportunity

In your presentation, this cues you to talk about the category growth, the performance of your brand, and the purpose of your call. You might say: "Last year, there was very significant growth in the category, with sales up over 40 percent. But the category leader was our brand, with growth more than twice the category average. Today, we're going to show you how to take advantage of this growth, which will give you an opportunity to increase your profits by as much as $50,000 next year...."

Similarly, visuals enable you to walk a customer through all the step-by-step details of your presentation. For example, let's say you were trying to sell a prospect on building a display to merchandise a product. Use a visual:

Retail              $109.95
Wholesale            85.00
Gross Profit        $ 24.95 (22.7%)
12/week               × 12
Profit/Week         $299.40
5' × 4'                 ÷ 20 square feet
               =    $14.97/sq. ft./wk.
               =    $778.44/sq. ft./yr.

Help your prospect understand your profit story by letting him or her see how you developed your numbers. For example: "You're currently selling this product for $109.95. That's yielding you a better-than-average margin of more than 22 percent. Almost $25 profit on every one you sell. In stores similar to yours, an extra display has increased those sales by 10 to 15 units a week. Let's say you sold just 12 more. That would mean almost $300 a week in extra profit from a display which is only five feet by four feet, or 20 square feet. For you, it means almost $15 extra profit per week, or over $778 per year, for every square foot. Tell me: Wouldn't you like every square foot in your store to return you $778 profit in the next year?"

The visual enables the prospect to see where your numbers come from while it lets you paraphrase the data with success stories and projected results. It guides you through the presentation without having to memorize numbers and details. Just remember: Keep those visuals clean and simple. Don't clutter them with too many details. Talk around them. *Never* read them.

# (3) Use Words and Phrases Designed to Create Vivid Images

This is a critical extra step in your feature–benefit sequence. You already know that you need to translate every product feature into a customer benefit. Now take that one step further by generating an image of the benefit. Like this:

"Our camcorder weighs only three pounds." (Feature)

"That means it's easy to use for almost anyone." (Benefit)

"Even your great-grandmother will be able to handle it. I'm sure she'll really enjoy taking pictures of you and the kids." (Image of the Benefit)

Or this:

"These mowers all have electronic ignition and an electric starter." (Feature)

"They start quickly, even on cold or damp days." (Benefit)

"You'll never again have to pull and pull and pull a starter cord 15 or 20 times to get your mower to start." (Image of the Benefit)

Think about it: When you were reading through those two examples, what was going through your mind? I'll bet there were images of a little old lady taking pictures of mom, dad, and the kids sharing good times on a beautiful afternoon. And a frustrated homeowner grunting and cursing at his recalcitrant lawn mower. Facts, words, and content don't arouse buying emotions. Images are the spark that ignites desire.

We think in pictures and images. Words are only an attempt to describe and re-create those pictures and images. Keep that in mind every time you speak to prospects. Don't just factually describe those features and benefits, but paint a picture in their minds which enables them to see themselves enjoying those benefits. Images. For you, the images of success.

# Secret 5:
# Help Them Make a Discovery

This is the follow-up step to the images of success. Yes, you first paint a picture in their minds. But next, you get them to *do* something which helps them discover the truth for themselves. Why? There are a few reasons. First off, just because you say something is so doesn't make it so in the minds of your prospects. They need evidence or personal experience that will constitute proof of your claim. And also, it is the nature of the selling process itself to move prospects to action, to buy. A passive prospect is not likely to suddenly spring to life at the end of the presentation and say, "You sold me. Where do I sign?" If you want to have your prospects alert and alive, ready to put their names on the dotted line at closing time, you've got to get them actively involved in the demonstration itself. When prospects participate in the presentation, they become part of the presentation. You get them in the act and on your side.

Help your prospects make discoveries by involving all of their senses. You started by creating a visual image in their minds. Now, let them see it, touch it, feel it, smell it, taste it, and do it. Even if they're just looking at or holding something.

Selling personal computers? Lead in with the features. Translate those features to benefits such as ease of use, flexibility, and quality of output. Then let them make a discovery. Hand them the power cord and say, "Let me show you what I mean. Here, plug this in. Good. Now, turn it on with that button there. OK, look at the screen. Choose whatever you'd like to do and press the key it says." Use active words and phrases—plug this in, turn it on, look at the screen, press the key—to involve their senses and encourage their participation.

And use these active words and phrases throughout your presentation, not just in the demonstration itself. For instance, if you were presenting a bar chart illustrating sales trends, don't say, "Sales were $56 million last year compared to $50 million the year before, an increase of 12 percent." That statement doesn't exactly stimulate senses, does it? Try this: "Look at what's happened to our sales in the last year. We went from $50 million to $56 million, an increase of 12 percent." It's alive, it's active, it tells your audience to *do* something.

Selling bedding and linens? The same thing applies: "These sheets have 110 threads per inch (feature). That makes them much smoother and more comfortable to sleep on (benefit). Feel this sample, and now compare that with this ordinary sheet which has only 80 threads per inch."

And remember the camcorder we were talking about. After creating the image of the family together enjoying the fellowship of taking pictures, hand a sample to the prospect: "Feel how light and well balanced it is. Now just look through the lens and press the button. There, you're making movies."

And the lawn mower: "Let me show you how easy this mower is to start. Turn that key to On. Now, set the throttle to High. That's it. All right, pull the cord one time and see what happens." At this point, of course, you take a deep breath and hope the mower immediately springs to life according to the script. If it does, you're primed for a close. If not, smile and keep a cool head. Certainly, as a professional salesperson you have planned and rehearsed your demonstration sequence and tested your model 30 times to be sure it absolutely, positively cranks on the first pull. That, however, is no guarantee of what will happen the thirty-first time. Think about that in advance. What can go wrong? What can you do to minimize the probability that something will go wrong? And how will you handle it to minimize the downside when, not if, that which could go wrong does go wrong? You might want to add that to your pre-approach preparation checklist.

# Secret 6:
# Close the Doors of Agreement That You Open

I don't want to get ahead of myself, since closing is the subject of the final chapter, but a few points are in order at this stage. As you will see, closing is not an isolated event which occurs at the end of your presentation. You do not say, in effect, "Well, that's the end of my presentation. If you don't have any more questions for me, then I have one for you: Can I have your order?" Closing is a process of building agreement throughout the presentation. What is often thought of as "the close" is merely the point at which you and the prospect reach agreement in principle to do business together.

In a way, a close is like a marriage proposal. If your goal was to win over that special someone, you likely invested considerable time presenting your features, translating them to benefits, and building the prospect's agreement that you were Mister or Miss Right. The proposal—the close—wasn't an event which occurred in isolation. It merely formalized, through specific commitments for action, the agreement you had built over weeks and months. The same thing in selling. Build agreement throughout the presentation and the close will be natural and effortless. Fail to nail down those points of agreement along the way and the close will be awkward and probably unsuccessful.

Creating images in the prospect's mind and helping them make a discovery will open the doors. Just be sure to close the doors you open. How? By asking questions to confirm the prospect's understanding and acknowledgement of the benefit.

Let's go back to some of the examples. After your prospect for the personal computer has discovered its ease of operation and quality output, close the doors:

> "Sure is easy to use this model, isn't it?"
> "How much time and money would it save you not to have to do that manually?"
> "I'll bet your secretary could get more and better work done for you with one of these, couldn't she?"

Get the bedding and linens prospects to feel the difference. Then close the door:

> "Doesn't that feel nice?"
> "Tell me, which one would *you* rather sleep on?"

The same principles apply with the camcorder and the lawn mower. State the feature, translate it to a benefit, create images in their minds, involve their senses to help them make a discovery, and confirm the benefit. And then, close the doors you opened with a question to gain agreement with the benefit and its importance. It's simple: If you tell prospects something, they may or may not believe it's true. If they see it, touch it, taste it, smell it, or do it, they probably believe it's true. But if they say it and acknowledge it, it's got to be true.

# Summing Up

In this chapter, we've explored the Six Top Secrets of show time, your presentation/demonstration. Let's review them:

- **Secret 1:** Clean up your room. Make sure the meeting room and meeting room arrangements are right. Check out the equipment and the lighting. All the right props in all their right places.

- **Secret 2:** Set the table with your opening. You wouldn't build a house on an inferior foundation. In selling, you build the foundation by getting the prospect's undivided attention at the beginning of the presentation. Get him or her away from distractions, get on the same wavelength, and establish rapport. When the relationship component feels right, make your opening statement and move into the presentation/demonstration.

- **Secret 3:** Are there any questions? Don't *you* talk. Get *them* to talk by your judicious use of questions. Talk less, listen more, sell more.

- **Secret 4:** Create images for success. Words don't sell because words don't communicate. People don't think in words, they think in images. Use words which create vivid images in their minds.

- **Secret 5:** Help them make a discovery. Do this by getting them to do something which involves all their senses to confirm the benefits of your product or service.

- **Secret 6:** Close the doors of agreement you open. Once the prospect has discovered those benefits, build agreement with a question which confirms understanding and acknowledges the benefit.

Sound easy? Sure does. That's because what we've discussed so far is the easy part. Dealing with customer resistance and working out the final details of a negotiated agreement are the tough parts—let's call them challenges—of a selling career and the focus of the final three chapters. So let's move on.

# Enhance Your Power Position in the Selling Situation

## The Seven Top Secrets of Power and Negotiation

Well, we're heading down the home stretch. Even though there are still three chapters to go, these last three chapters are closely interrelated, and all address the same basic point: closing a profitable sale. In this chapter, we'll look at power and negotiation to see how the professional salesperson enhances his or her power position in the selling situation, then recognizes and applies negotiation skills to arrive at a mutually beneficial agreement. Chapter Seven deals specifically with objections. But think about it: Aren't objections really just points of disagreement that one deals with through discussion and negotiation? And Chapter Eight is about closing. If you're in a strong power position, know how to negotiate, and can effectively deal with the prospect's objections, you're already closing, aren't you?

As you read through the final three chapters, keep this in mind:

> Closing a profitable sale, handling objections, and negotiating agreement from a position of strength are not isolated elements in the sales presentation. They're all woven together as part of a *process*.

That's important, so let's repeat: Dealing with objections, negotiating the details, and closing the sale with the customer's name on the dotted line are not isolated events but part of a *process* in play throughout the sales encounter.

In this chapter we'll begin to understand this process with the Seven Top Secrets of Power and Negotiation. First of all, we'll explore the nature of power in the sales situation and how you can enhance your power position. Then we'll take a look at the negotiation process. Just like salesmanship, negotiation is a skill. To negotiate effectively, you must know the secrets of starting strong out of the gate, getting all issues on the table, and tying it all together.

# Secret 1:
# Know What Power Is

Power is, simply, the ability to get someone to do something they wouldn't do otherwise. In selling, that means buying from you instead of someone else; initialing an agreement today instead of checking with your competitor tomorrow; agreeing to your price of 30¢ instead of the 25¢ they originally asked for or the 28¢ they hoped to get.

Some people seem uncomfortable when I discuss selling in terms of a power game. My suggestion to them is to book the next flight out and take up residence on another planet! *Life* is a power game and power is an essential component of interpersonal communication. Remember the point we discussed in Chapter Three about power and assertiveness. They are always being played out in any communication.

To a large extent, power is derived from one party's ability to reward or punish the other. The carrot and the stick. Now, ask yourself: On what basis will a customer—or anyone—determine whether to reward you, punish you, or do nothing? Sure, a lot of factors come into play, but it all comes down to one thing: enlightened self-interest. That customer will sign the order form this minute, or will drag out the negotiations for weeks and months, or will show you the door and phone your competitor for one reason: It's in his or her best interest to do so.

In a selling situation, your cause is lost at the outset if you convey the impression that you really need the sale and that you need the customer more than he or she needs you and your product. Power up to negotiate! By what you say and how you say it, consciously convey your confidence that the *customer* needs *you* and what you sell.

You may not like this and you may not think it's fair. Well, the world has never been fair and you don't have to like it. But it's a fact that customers are *never* going to close if they feel your need to sell is greater than their need to buy. Customers are *never* going to close if they perceive themselves to be in a superior power position. And why should they close? Why should they agree to your proposal when they know you need the sale so badly? All they have to do is sit tight and bide their time because they know you'll make a concession before you'd turn and walk away. How can you expect to close them if they believe they hold the power and can force you down a penny or two?

In any transaction, the buyer wants all the benefits, yes, but wants them all at the lowest possible price. Closing is often described as getting customer commitment to buy. That's not enough. Commitment to buy is one thing, but agreement on terms and conditions is something else. Depending on the power dynamics, the customer may offer 50 percent of your list price or 50 percent over your list price. Whatever the price, terms, and conditions, the final agreement is *always* of mutual benefit. If the price is too high to be of benefit to the customer, agreement is impossible. The buyer says no and means it. Similarly, if the price is too low to be of benefit to the salesperson, he or she will walk away. Two things can happen: First, the highest price acceptable to the customer is less than the lowest price acceptable to the salesperson. Result: No deal. But more often what happens is that there is a range of prices within which it is in the best interest of both parties to reach agreement. And where you wind up on that range—high side or low side—will be determined by the perceived power positions of the respective parties.

There is one little word which may have snuck past you unnoticed: *perceived* power positions. Although certain manifestations of power are quantifiable, power itself is an intangible. Perception is reality. Just ask any adept poker player or the principals in any threatened diplomatic or military encounter. In a selling situation, you may falsely assume that you, the seller, are in an inferior power position. Certainly any experienced buyer will do their best to convince you that is so. But it probably isn't so. If you've done your homework and understand all the features and benefits, you should know that the prospect needs you as much as you need that prospect. Not convinced? Then you're not ready to make the sales call. You still have some more preparation to do.

Also in this section, I've cited examples of price as the major focus in the power game. Certainly price is important, but it's by no means the only point or even the most important point at issue. Recall our earlier discussion of price versus value. Lower price or build *value*. Your best tactic is probably not to lower price but to identify and present other satisfiers which will build value. That raises the customer threshold of an acceptable price. And that means you'll come out better.

# Secret 2:
# Create Power Within Yourself

You can create power for yourself in the selling encounter. In fact, you yourself are the most important power resource. The prime credo: Knowledge is Power! In the early pages of this book, we noted the need for the professional salesperson to know everything possible about the product, customer, competition, and industry. Do your homework before the call. And in the presentation, utilize questions to learn more about the customer—needs, buying motives, and hot button. Isn't that only common sense? The more you know about your product, the better you're able to identify benefits and present them as a competent, knowledgeable expert. The more you know about your customer's business—operations, policies, and procedures—the better you're able to determine the impact those benefits will have on the business. That not only builds agreement, it builds value. And knowing how your customers do business enables you to develop proposals which fit within their systems and their budgets. Knowing the relative strengths and weaknesses of the competition helps you focus on the unique selling points to emphasize in your presentation. And industry knowledge enhances your power of expertise. Your role is no longer that of "just a salesperson" but one of a consultant, expert, and partner. Without the consultant's attendant fees, of course. That builds your value to your customers and makes it to their benefit to do business with you. Even though your prices are a little higher than your less knowledgeable competitor.

Knowledge is the foundation of power in selling. Without it, you're nowhere. With it, the sky is the limit. You're confident because you're ready. You're prepared. And then your nonverbal cues convey an impression of professionalism, power, and confidence. It is critical to remember that everything you've learned about nonverbal communication and impression formation won't amount to a hill of beans if you're not totally knowledgeable and prepared. You may open with those good gestures, posture, eye contact, and all the rest, but you'll quickly look like a whipped dog when they raise points or ask questions you're unprepared for.

Another way the power is within you is through you, yourself. If you're a decent person who behaves courteously and ethically, chances are people will like you. And if people like and respect you, they'll be more inclined to do business with you and even make concessions they wouldn't make to someone else. So, yes, be tough on the issues and project an impression of power and confidence. But be nice—someone your customer can identify with and the kind of person business professionals like doing business with.

Finally, your attitude and personality can also enhance your perceived power. Genuine enthusiasm is a must. It starts with belief in your product and pride in your company. You build on that by demonstrating to your prospect that his or her business is important to you. Let the prospect know you want this business and will work hard before and after the sale. Be persistent. Don't accept a "No," either in your request for an appointment or in your attempt to close the sale. Come back, come back, and come back! Just don't become obnoxious about it. Consider a "No" to mean that apparently you have failed to communicate the need for the prospect to say "Yes." The power of persistence can work for you, but only when it's coupled with the attitude that your prospect really needs your product or service. The power of persistence will be ineffective if it's coupled with the attitude that you really need this sale in order to make your mortgage payment the first of the month. You *want* the business because the prospect *needs* your benefits. But you don't have to have this sale and are prepared to take a walk if acceptable terms and conditions can't be worked out. That's the power of risk taking. If you're unwilling or unable to walk away from the table, your prospect will just sit there ticking off one concession after another. Serious negotiations often don't get started until one of the parties gets up and announces, "I'm sorry, but it doesn't look like we'll be able to get together. My last offer is the very best I can do." And at that, begins to pack up the briefcase. That signals to the other party that this is as good a deal as he or she is likely to get and that he or she is about to lose out on it. Chances are good your prospect will say something like, "Well, now, let's take one more look at this." It might be said right then and there, it might be said as you both walk out to the parking lot, or you might get a call two or three days later when the prospect is finally convinced you really were ready to take a walk. Then, and only then, do you get down to the little nitty-gritty points that finalize agreement on all the issues.

# Secret 3:
# Tap Into Other Sources
# of Power

Yes, you are your own best power resource. But there are other sources of power you can tap in the selling situation. Let's look at them one at a time.

# The Customer Gives You Power

Part of this source of power is your customer knowledge. A thorough knowledge of the customer, the business, problems/needs/opportunities, and that customer's way of doing business gives you, as we've noted, the power to properly focus your selling effort. Along those lines, knowing the customer's buying style and all the buying influences helps you fine tune your tactics.

We've emphasized the importance of knowledge and information in building power. Asking questions and carefully listening to the prospect. The problem is, though, that in your presentation the prospect will tend to be very circumspect about conveying information that will enhance your power position at their expense. Don't expect them to interrupt your presentation and say, "You're right. Your product is better. It's well worth the 50 percent higher price than the competition. In fact, we've done studies which indicate it would be a bargain at twice the price. We wouldn't consider buying from someone else. And, we only have a ten-day supply left. We won't have to pay extra to get a thousand in by next week, I hope."

Of course they're not going to tell you that, but it sure would be helpful to know, wouldn't it? To get that sort of information, remember two things:

(1) Get it far in advance of your presentation and negotiation. The closer you get to the event, the harder information is to come by.

(2) Get it from secretaries, foremen, operators, and other user influences. They're the people who *really* know what's going on in most companies. And also from your technical people who, due to your competence and foresight, have established a relationship and partnership with *their* technical people.

Naturally, never let anyone know all you know or how you came to know it. They may hit you with, "We have a tough time reconciling a price 50 percent higher than the competition. You're just going to have to do better than that if you want to do business with us." When you know you're in the catbird seat, with your best poker face look them in the eye and say, "You're right, our price is higher. But companies who have conducted studies confirm our experience that despite the higher price, our product is of better quality and that results in lower total operating cost. I wish I could lower the price but I just can't do it. We only have one shipment left, and if you don't want it, someone else has agreed to buy it." Now, just what do you think is going to happen next? Will that customer really permit you to walk through that door? Of course not!

Some people get a little uneasy when I cite such examples to illustrate knowledge and power in negotiation. They feel it's unethical not to put all your cards on the table and let the prospect know everything there is to know about you and everything you know about them. It doesn't present an ethical dilemma to me. This is the way it is. This is how the game is played.

There is another potential source of power from your customer, often overlooked. When selling in the business-to-business environment, generally you'll focus on benefits for the prospect's company: better profits, lower costs, and the like. But don't stop there. Also consider personal benefits to the prospect within his or her company. Most prospects are interested in looking good within their own organizations. They want to avoid hassles and risks. Like all of us, they're probably under time constraints and would like to get the buying decision over with so they can move on to other business. That gives you power. Sure, they'll tell you they can meet with your competitor to see if they can get a better price; but that will take time, maybe days or weeks, that they don't have to spare. Point out to them how good they'll look buying a reliable product from you which provides needed benefits to their company, even at a slightly higher price. Compare that to the downside risk of a less expensive competitor failing to provide all those benefits. And balance the potential positive recognition of them saving a few pennies against the potential negative blame of buying the cheaper item and having it come up short. When a buyer sees personal benefits—as well as benefits for the company—in dealing with you, the customer enhances your power.

# The Competition Gives You Power

The first side of this equation is obvious. The more you know about the competition—their strengths and their weaknesses—the better you're able to focus your presentation on your strengths and respective benefits. The other side of the equation, though not as obvious, is: Create competition! No, I don't mean bring in other suppliers to compete with you for the customer's business. I *do* mean to convey that other customers are competing with your prospect to procure your products and services. I'll go into this in more detail in the last chapter, but will make a few top-line comments here.

Basically, it's just human nature to not want something no one else wants, and to want something others want. If your prospect believes no one else is competing for your product, why should they want it? And if they believe the same item will be available tomorrow at the same price or less, what's their incentive to buy today? You gain the power to motivate your prospect to make a buying decision now when you create competition for whatever you have. Just be sure that the "competition" is credible in the mind of the prospect and be willing to walk away if the buyer can't compete with this competition.

# Your Company Gives You Power

Or doesn't, as the case may be. What's your company's reputation for quality and service? Reliability and workmanship? Follow-up after the sale? If your company passes muster on all that and more, it gives you power as their representative. You may be a freshly graduated 22-year-old puppy, but think of the power you hold calling on a prospect representing a company like IBM. Just imagine the difference in your power on a customer call if you represented _____. (You fill in the blank.)

The power of commitment cannot be faked. If your company has a good reputation and commands respect, and if you honestly believe in your company and its products, you'll be committed. Genuine commitment is persuasive. The flip side: If you're not sold on the company or its products, how can you expect to sell someone else? If you don't believe your company has integrity, how much integrity can you have by representing them? Commitment is essential to success in anything. Your company, through its practices and products, must provide you the power of commitment. If they can't, don't, or won't, quit.

Another way your company gives you power is through authority. More precisely, through the *lack* of authority. You might think you'd be better off if you had considerable latitude in negotiating prices, terms, and other details. Probably not. You're actually likely to close more sales, in far less time, by having *less* authority. With unlimited authority to set prices and terms, for example, you could spend half a day wrangling out the details. Contrast that with having to tell your prospect, "I'm sorry, but there's nothing I can do about that. The pricing schedule is set by headquarters, and we offer the same prices and terms to all our customers." Attendant to this lack of authority, your company provides you with the power of legitimacy, or the power of the printed word.

Printed words carry more weight and authority than spoken words. It's one thing to tell a customer that your price is 40¢ a pound and that you can't offer them 38¢ unless they take at least 10,000 pounds, but that you can make it 37¢ if they take 100,000. It's something else to show that to a customer on a printed page.

There is one final point on lack of authority and the power of legitimacy. As in other matters, there can be too much of a good thing. Yes, it's good to have clear, specific policies laid out in writing. No, you do not want a lack of flexibility in determining the details of an agreement. Your chances for making an agreement are enhanced if you can generate a wide variety of possibilities within specified parameters. Let the prospect determine which combination best suits their needs. And if you make a particular arrangement with a customer, be sure you write it up as an arrangement option for all your other customers in the future. You may think you can cut a deal with one customer and that your other customers won't ever find out about it, and that you don't even have to bring it up when you call on those other customers. But you are wrong. Of course they'll all find out about that deal and want the same one.

# Secret 4:
# Know What Negotiation Is

Negotiation is interpersonal communication directed at achieving a mutually satisfactory agreement on specified points. As communication, it consists of content and relationship, power and assertiveness. I emphasize power and assertiveness. If, as is likely the case, there is a range in the parameters where both parties could reach agreement, power and assertiveness will determine at which end of the range the final accord is made. For example, A is selling his house and feels he will take no less than $80,000. B is interested in buying it and would pay as much as $85,000. There is a range—$80,000 to $85,000—over which agreement is possible. But what will be the final price? $80,000? $85,000? $82,500? It depends on the power, real or perceived, of the respective parties.

First of all, let's be sure we understand the background to the negotiation situation. Negotiation starts when the seller has submitted an initial proposal and both parties have reached agreement in principal. That is to say, they've agreed to agree, but now must hunker down to iron out the terms, conditions, and other specifics of the final agreement. Think about that for a moment. That means the sale has been closed—or sort of closed. Traditionally, books on selling focus heavily on closing. That's all well and good if there's no latitude in price or other points. The seller presents the product and its benefits; builds agreement; asks a closing question. The buyer accepts. End of story. That may happen in a few circumstances, but not in most. Generally, after the "close" there are numerous details to be worked out. And it's power, information, and negotiation skills which make the difference between closing a sale and closing a profitable sale. See what I mean about why you can't look at negotiation and closing in isolation?

Let's go through a typical negotiation situation. John Jarrett is a sales representative for Telstar Telecommunications, a firm which specializes in the sales and service of business office telephone systems. He's just presented a proposal to Beth Bennett of the Consolidated Cupcake Corporation. The package includes equipment, employee orientation and training, and a one-year service contract. As we join them, John asks a closing question and the parties achieve agreement in principal. Then, they proceed to iron out the specific terms and conditions.

> John: Wouldn't you agree, then, that Telstar Telecommunications is the best company for your needs?
>
> Beth: Yes, I'm impressed with what you've shown me. I did have one question, though: What was your total cost figure again?
>
> John: $50,000.
>
> Beth: Hmm. That's a bit on the high side. Let me ask you this: If we liked your system and decided to go with a similar package in our five branch offices next year, you could probably give us some kind of a quantity discount, couldn't you?
>
> John: Yes. We could do it for $46,000 per office.
>
> Beth: Then we're looking at a price of $46,000 if we just do this office, right?
>
> John: All right. We'll go ahead and do it for $46,000.

Beth:    Still, I'm afraid that's more than we can handle. You've just got to do better than $46,000.

John:    Well, $44,000 is about as low as we could go.

Beth:    All I have in the budget is $40,000.

John:    There's just no way we can do it for that. It's below our cost.

Beth:    All right, let me suggest this. I'll do you a favor. I can squeeze as much as $2,000 out of my travel budget. Let's say we split the difference and ink the deal: $42,000. I wish I could do better, John, but I can't. There is no more. It's that or nothing.

John:    Well, I guess something is better than nothing.

Beth:    Great. Then we're agreed on $42,000. We'll pay that in full in six months.

John:    Six months? But our terms are net 30 days.

Beth:    That's going to present a problem. How about the first 50 percent in 60 days?

John:    All right. And the balance in six months. Can we begin installation week after next?

Beth:    No, we need to have it fully operational by Monday morning.

John:    But we don't have that equipment in inventory. It's all shipped out of El Paso. If I place the order today, it'll be late next week before it arrives.

Beth:    Well, fly it here overnight. Call one of the air freight companies. Shipping arrangements are your problem. You *can* get it here to install everything over the weekend, then, can't you.

John:    It's *possible* to do it, but I don't...

Beth:    Fine. You can do the installation over the weekend.

John:     It *can* be done, but ...

Beth:    Good. Just one last thing: We'll expect you to throw in the three-year warranty and service. We're not going to pay extra for the second and third years.

John:   But the extended service contract is normally $2,000 extra. The basic contract is for one year. I've already lowered the price by $8,000. How can I throw in another $2,000?

Beth:   All right, I'll meet you halfway. Just throw in the second year. That's a reasonable compromise, isn't it?

John:   I suppose so. Is there anything else?

Beth:   No, I think that's it. I'll write up a summary of our discussion for my manager to consider. Can you meet with him tomorrow morning at 9?

John:   You can't initial our agreement today?

Beth:   No, I'm just here to get your initial proposal. You'll need to meet with him to negotiate the final price, terms, and conditions.

John:   Negotiate…the…final…terms…and…conditions…

Beth:   Yes. His name is Dan Davis. He'll be expecting you at 9:00.

Empathize with John? Been there a time or two yourself? As you can see from this example, there's a little more to the end game of selling than just closing or reaching agreement in principle. John closed the sale and confirmed the agreement. Unfortunately for him, Beth, a skilled negotiator, tore him apart working out all the details. Poor John was in an inferior power position from the start, and things only got worse. His knowledge, prospecting skills, and selling skills got him the appointment and persuaded the customer to buy, but all he built up was unraveled because of his ineptitude at negotiation.

Got a feel for what negotiation is? Good. Now let's look at the next three top secrets of effective negotiation and see how this situation might have been handled differently.

# Secret 5:
# Start Out From a Position of Strength

Whatever you're negotiating, it's essential to start out on the right foot. If you enter the proceedings with a weak posture or stumble trying to get out of the gate, it's unlikely you'll recover.

Any negotiation starts with the respective parties having a general impression of their strength and the strength of the other side. Knowledge, of course, is the key. You hope you have every fact there is about them. You hope they don't have every fact there is about you. Realistically, though, no one knows everything there is to know about anyone. Therefore, starting strong out of the gate, conveying an image of strength and confidence, can cause the other party to perceive that perhaps your position is a little stronger than they thought it was. The opposite happens if you open weakly. The result: A strong opening and the other side's expectations drop a little. A weak opening and they go up.

Keep in mind that the opening of the negotiation process is not the moment when the parties begin discussing points of agreement in a formal bargaining session. In truth, the negotiation may have begun days, weeks, or months sooner, in apparently innocent discussions or preliminary conversations. Listen carefully to pick up on information or deadlines facing the other side. Learn the skill of shutting up so as not to convey knowledge about your situation which could endanger your position later on. And even when the formal session begins, there will be at least a few minutes before the parties get down to content issues. Use those moments to build your relationship component and be aware of your nonverbal communication. Project an impression of neutrality, an attitude of confidence that their need to buy is as great as your need to sell.

You may not anticipate closing your initial proposal as it stands, but set your sights on that objective anyhow. Aim high and you'll probably come out better. Let yourself be intimidated into initially retreating and you're probably headed for trouble.

There are few, if any, situations in which one party or the other holds all the cards. I guess the Allies were in that position in the spring of 1945: Unconditional surrender, nothing less! It hasn't happened much in international politics since then. I can think of a few situations personally where I thought at the time that I—or they—held all the power.

You too? Consider such circumstances, though, and generally you'll see that even though one side held a disproportionate amount of power, there was not just one, and only one, possible outcome. If there's a range of outcomes, there's an opportunity for negotiation.

If there's an opportunity for negotiation, be sure you open the process conveying strength. Ask yourself:

- Is there anything I could do or not do that would benefit the other side?

- Is there anything I could do or refuse to do that would *hurt* the other side?

If your answer to either question is "Yes," the other side has reason to negotiate with you. That means you have strength, perhaps more than you thought you had. In any case, convey to them that you do have more strength than they thought you had.

A final thought on the power opening. You may be thinking, "Yeah, sure, I'll start off smiling, confident, eye contact, good handshake, and all, but I gotta make a deal. I know that, they know that. I can't just walk away from this." Or *can* you walk away? Remember the power of risk taking. If you *can't* walk away, all they have to do is wait you out and it's unconditional surrender. No matter how badly you want to make a deal, don't enter the fray before figuring the downside risk of failing to achieve a settlement. How bad can it be? What are your alternatives to reaching an agreement?

Think about it. You probably do have alternatives. Failing to come to terms here and now today is probably not the end of the world. Knowing that should enhance your power and give you a better start out of the gate. At the very least, it gives you a standard against which a possible agreement can be measured, a point beyond which you just won't go.

Go back to the scenario between John and Beth, and you'll see how John stumbled out of the gate. After achieving agreement in principal, Beth asked him to clarify his price: $50,000. She then did a "What if" on him: What if they took five instead of one? John quoted $46,000. Beth responded, predictably, by demanding the quantity price on the single system, and what happened? John initially retreated. The power scale had tipped in Beth's favor. John never recovered from his weak opening. Beth, with one unilateral concession under her belt, repeated the process. John, weakly attempting to hold the deal together, kept retreating. Beth, the adept negotiator, kept hammering away.

Establish a strong posture at the opening. Start strong out of the gate.

# Secret 6:
# Get All Issues and Points on the Table

This top secret is an essential for effective negotiation, and it's where most salespeople get into trouble. And it's just common sense if you think about it. The unskilled negotiator grinds through each and every point of agreement, one at a time. Each issue—price, terms, delivery, peripherals, etc., etc., etc.—is ironed out in isolation. There are three problems in trying to work out an agreement that way.

First of all, the process is going to take forever. There may be dozens—or hundreds—of points to be addressed. For each item, the respective sides are some distance apart in their initial positions. That means both parties must find an acceptable point each can live with between those positions. To get there, one side, the other, or probably both will have to make a concession. That's going to take a lot of time. And you have to be able to find acceptable middle ground on each and every point. If there's just one issue you can't get together on, the deal is dead. And after making concessions and haggling over twenty or thirty points, the respective sides are bound to hit something where both of them decide to draw the line in the sand and say, "No, I won't give on that one." Impasse.

Secondly, dealing with each item in isolation—piecemealing—creates a win–lose negotiation situation. If, for example, you agree to lower your price, the other side wins at your expense. If they agree to pay your price, you've won at their expense. If you meet somewhere in between, both of you have lost something and gotten nothing in return, except the opportunity to move on to another point and continue the win–lose process. This is not exactly conducive to building agreement. One side, or probably both, starts to feel they've conceded enough. Agreement becomes progressively difficult on successive points.

Finally, piecemealing is inappropriate because the individual points of agreement do not exist in isolation. They're all part of a *package* which has to be worked out. Let's look at price. Of course price is a major focus of negotiation, but it's not an isolated element. Your price will vary depending on terms, quantity, packaging, and other variables. You shouldn't be trying to agree on price separately and quantity separately because price and quantity are interrelated.

Don't piecemeal. Instead, get *all* the issues and points on the table *before* you start negotiating. Take notes. Ask questions. Probe to identify all the points on which agreement must be achieved. Maintain close attention and *listen*. Get a sense of the other party's *real* needs and objectives. Look behind their stated position on individual issues. Keep asking: "Is there anything else we need to address?" Write down each and every point they'd like to talk about. Express a willingness to discuss anything, but make no commitment before getting the complete shopping list.

Let's go back and see how well John did at getting everything on the table in his negotiation with Beth. First, as we saw, Beth raised the issue of price. John weakly attempted to get the variable of quantity on the table, but then retreated and made a unilateral concession. This was the turning point in their discussion. What John should have done was to take notes to identify *all* the issues before negotiating on *any* issues: "Yes, we'll need to talk about price and quantity. Is there anything else?" Of course, there was: Terms, installation, delivery. All of those points, which affected costs for John's company, should have been put on the table along with price and quantity, and dealt with as a package. Instead, what happened? First, Beth, emboldened by receiving a unilateral concession of $4,000 on the price, decided to go for another one. And success! John gave her another $2,000. He'd dropped his price from $50,000 to $44,000, with nothing to show for it. Understandably, Beth opted to continue piecemealing on price, employing the tactic of telling him that $40,000 was as high as she could go since that was all she had in her budget. John piecemealed the price to $42,000. And Beth proceeded to play the same game on each and every variable in isolation. John continued to concede, likely obliterating any profit on the deal for his company, hoping in vain that one more concession would be his last and that he could hold the deal together.

This is important, so let's repeat:

- Don't piecemeal!

- Don't deal with points in isolation!

- Don't make unilateral concessions!

- *Do* get everything on the table *before* you start to negotiate!

# Secret 7:
# Tie the Package All Together

Effective negotiation can begin only after all the issues have been put on the table. As we've noted, that means at the outset getting the complete shopping list of points of concern. Then, continuing to search for new variables by brainstorming a wide variety of options. Why keep searching for variables? Because the more items you have on the table, the better your chances of assembling a package which will be acceptable to both parties. And remember: Keep the whole package in mind, not just its individual components.

The reason you get as much as possible on the table before you start to negotiate is because of a concept called the relativity of variables. That is to say, a small concession for one party on an issue maybe of substantial benefit to the other party. Effective negotiation results in *both* parties making a small concession and getting a large benefit in return. That's win–win. Let's look at an example which, to keep things simple, involves only two variables, price and terms.

Party A is selling some land for an asking price of $10,000. Terms are 50 percent at closing, 50 percent three years later. Party B is interested in buying. If they negotiate piecemeal, they first talk price. B offers $9,000. A says he'll sell for $9,600. B counters with $9,400. They agree on $9,500. Now, what just happened? A, negotiating piecemeal, just lowered the price $500 *and got nothing in return*. A fundamental of negotiation is that you *always* get something in return when making a concession.

So what's going to happen next? B is going to say he wants to pay just 20 percent at closing and 80 percent *five* years later. They finally agree on 35 percent at closing and 65 percent four years later. Again, A has made a concession.

If you're the buyer, piecemealing can be an effective tactic since it can coerce the other side into making unilateral concessions. As the seller, piecemealing is a prescription for disaster. So what should A do? Tie it all together! If B makes an offer of $9,000, A might counter by saying he'd take $9,000 if B paid 100 percent at closing. B says he only wants to pay 20 percent at closing. A counters by saying he'd want $11,000 with only 20 percent at closing.

An impasse? Not at all! Keep searching for variables! A might suggest that he'd take either $10,000 with 20 percent at closing or $9,000 with

50 percent at closing *if* B will give him a non-refundable deposit of $1,000 in cash today, the remaining down payment to be made in cash at a closing to be held within no more than 10 days.

See what I'm driving at? Every time you indicate a willingness to make a concession, tie it to something you get in return. Also remember to provide the buyer with a variety of alternatives, all of which are equally acceptable to you. Depending on the relativity of variables for the buyer, he can determine which is more important: lower price or better terms. In fact, if the buyer has plenty of cash, he might just counter by offering a non-refundable deposit of $2,000 in cash today and 100 percent of the remainder in cash at closing *if* A will accept a price of $7,500. In this scenario, B might enhance his power by pulling cash out of his pocket and saying, "Take it or leave it. Do you want to initial this contract or not?" That's the sort of thing that makes negotiation such a fun game. Two can play, and both can walk away feeling they won.

A word on agreeing to concessions: Don't make them too readily. Even if you're chomping at the bit to say "Yes," take a moment or two as if to ponder. Make it look like it hurts. The reason is simple. If you agree too quickly, the other party will decide they could have done better if they'd tried. No matter how good a deal they got, they won't be happy. The agreement may even unravel. I have a personal illustration. I was trying to sell a house a few years ago. I'd been living at a new location, 400 miles away, for over six months. My asking price was realistic at $49,900, but I was so anxious to sell I'd decided I wasn't about to let a serious buyer get away, even if I could get as little as $40,000. One blessed day, a buyer called and made an offer: $40,000 on the nose. My reaction to myself was to jump up and down with glee. But did I just come out and say "Sold"? Certainly not. I hemmed and hawed, and said there was no way I could go that low. I asked about the buyer's finances and when he was prepared to close. He said he had cash and could close in seven days. I said that if he could close the next week with all cash at closing, I could go as low as $42,000. He countered with $41,000. I came back and said I'd accept the $41,000 only if I could keep the drapes. It was a deal. The bottom line: I wound up with $1,000 and a set of drapes more than I was prepared to go. And the buyer was happier because he believed he'd pushed me about as far as I was willing to go. In fact, he even came back a few days before closing to confirm that by asking for a few more concessions. I declined, saying that I was obligated to proceed as we'd agreed, but if he wanted out of that agreement, it was fine with me. This is the power of risk taking. He closed.

You may think the best way to keep a deal together is to agree to demands to make concessions. The opposite is more likely. Demanding at least *something* in return, or refusing to go any further, will generally be more effective in tying the whole package together.

With all this in mind, let's revisit the negotiation between Telstar Telecommunications and Consolidated Cupcake, and see how it could have turned out differently. Instead of John, the Telstar sales rep is Roz Ramirez. And Roz knows the top secrets of power and negotiation.

Roz: Wouldn't you agree, then, that Telstar Telecommunications is the best company for your needs?

Beth: Yes, I'm impressed with what you've shown me. What was your total cost figure again?

Roz: $50,000.

Beth: Hmmm. That's a bit on the high side. Let me ask you this: If we liked your system and decided to go with a similar package in our five branch offices next year, you could probably give us some kind of a quantity discount, couldn't you?

Roz: It's something we could talk about. (Making a notation on her order form) Is there anything else you were wondering about?

Beth: Yes. What did you say your payment terms were?

Roz: Net 30 days.

Beth: That's going to present a problem. I'm not going to have next year's budget for another six months.

Roz: (Making a notation) So we'll need to talk about payment terms. What else will we need to discuss?

Beth: Delivery and set-up. We need to have it fully operational by Monday morning.

Roz: (Making a notation) Delivery and set-up. Any other points we need to finalize?

Beth: One more thing: We'll expect you to throw in the three-year warranty and service.

Roz: (Making a notation) Then we'll need to discuss the warranty and service provision. Have we omitted anything, or is this all we need to agree on?

Beth: I believe that will do it.

Roz:    Well, let's see where we are. You were saying you
        wished to make payment in six months instead of
        30 days. If we could help you out on the price,
        could you pay at least half within 30 days?

Beth:   We could talk about it.

Roz:    Fine. Now, you said you wanted everything
        installed by Monday morning. That's going to give
        us some logistical challenges. We don't have this
        equipment in inventory and will have to truck it
        from El Paso. That means it should get here late
        next week.

Beth:   Call one of the air freight companies, then.
        They'll have it here tomorrow. How you get it
        here is your problem. Just get it here.

Roz:    If you want us to do that, that's what we'll do. But
        the cost would be prohibitive. That's *our* problem,
        because every dollar spent on transport is a dollar
        you can't save on total price. And from what you
        were saying, wouldn't a savings on total price be
        worth a week?

Beth:   If transport cost savings were reflected in the total
        price, we can live with it.

Roz:    Then let me ask you this: Don't you weekly send
        your trucks west to L.A. on Interstate 10 through
        El Paso? Coming back empty?

Beth:   Yes. What are you driving at?

Roz:    Just this: If one of your trucks could stop at our El
        Paso warehouse on the way back, we can save *all*
        the shipping costs. When's the next one going
        through?

Beth:   Day after tomorrow. And arriving back next
        Wednesday.

Roz:    (Making notations on her order form and punch-
        ing in some numbers on her calculator) Tell me
        what you think of this. Your trucks transport all
        the equipment from El Paso. Week after next, we
        begin installation here. Under those arrange-
        ments, we can give you one system for $47,000. If

you choose to place similar systems in your five
branch offices, they would qualify for a volume
discount and would be $45,000 each. That would
be with terms of 50 percent within 10 days and
the remainder in six months. With the three-year
warranty and service contract, add $2,000 per
system.

Beth:   So you're saying a total of $47,000 per system.

Roz:    $49,000 for one system and $47,000 each for the
next five.

Beth:   I can't go along with paying an extra $2,000 for
the first system, and I don't like having to pay an
extra $2,000 for that warranty.

Roz:    I understand how you feel. Let me ask you this: If
we could give you a price of $45,000 per system,
regardless of how many you purchase, including a
*two*-year warranty, would you be able to initial a
purchase order requisition today?

Beth:    Make it $45,000 with a *three*-year warranty and
you're on.

Roz:    Hmm. That's a rock bottom price. I don't know.
Tell me this: If I could do that, could you cut a
check for the first 50 percent today instead of in
10 days.

Beth:   If I call Accounting now, they can have you a
check in 30 minutes.

Roz:    Then I believe we're together on everything. If
you'll just initial this agreement here, we're ready
to go.

Beth:   (Signing the agreement) I need to call Accounting.

Quite a difference. And why? Because Roz asked questions, focused
on customer benefits, and she knew the Seven Top Secrets of Power and
Negotiation.

# Summing Up

This chapter addressed the first of three components of the end-game of the sales call: power and negotiation. We'll look at the other two components—objections and closing—in the final two chapters.

Let's review the Seven Top Secrets of Power and Negotiation:

- **Secret 1:** Knowing what power is and the role power plays in the selling situation.

- **Secret 2:** The power is within you. Be sure to convey an impression of strength and confidence.

- **Secret 3:** Others give you power. Make sure you know who those others are, and how they can enhance your power position.

- **Secret 4:** Know what negotiation is and develop those effective negotiation skills.

- **Secret 5:** Start out from a position of strength.

- **Secret 6:** Get everything on the table *before* you try to iron out individual points. And, as you discuss points of agreement, don't piecemeal. That's because you should deal with all those points as a package, not in isolation.

- **Secret 7:** Tie the package all together in a mutually beneficial agreement.

Beginning to feel confident? Good, because it's time to move on to Part Two of the end-game trilogy, what every salesperson hates but should learn to love: Objections.

# CHAPTER 7

# Objections Are Your Friends

---

## The Five Top Secrets of Overcoming Objections

You may have been a bit surprised by the title of this chapter. Objections are your *friends*? But yes, it's true, though it is one of the best kept "top secrets" of selling.

If you're already a successful sales professional, you probably know that handling objections effectively is the key to making a sale. On the other hand, if you're just getting started in sales, you may fear objections, believing them to be only obstacles to be overcome. The fact is, objections are your friends. Do you still find that hard to believe? Then consider this: Without objections, you don't have a job. Without objections, all your company would have to do is hire a staff to answer the phone and take orders.

Overcoming objections is the heart and soul of professional selling. It is *the* most important selling skill. Doing your homework and being prepared is necessary and important. Involving your prospect and making an effective presentation is necessary and important. And negotiation and closing skills are necessary and important. But handling objections is the key and, as we'll see, objections are points of negotiation which can help close the sale.

In this chapter, we'll address the Five Top Secrets of Overcoming Objections and making them your friends. The first of these is the magic word—*listen*. Listen carefully to the prospect's objection before you respond. Then classify the objection. If it's relationship-based, shift the discussion toward content. But if it's content-based, skillful handling of the objection will lead you directly into the close.

# Secret 1:
# Listen Before You Respond
# to Objections

Heard that word before, haven't you? We've already described the importance of asking questions and actively listening, rather than just running your mouth. However, it's important to re-emphasize the importance of listening when dealing with objections. Let's face it, when your prospects are objecting, they're not exactly telling you things you want to hear. Objections are seldom confused with statements of satisfaction indicating a willingness to buy. The prospect is saying your product isn't good enough or is too expensive, that the company is satisfied with your competitor who has better products at a lower price. Or that he or she likes the way things are done now and sees no need to change. So, what's your impulsive reaction to such a customer statement? Right! An immediate response. And that's just the *wrong* thing to do when a customer hits you with an objection.

The first secret to making objections your friends is to resist the temptation to speak. Instead, encourage prospects to talk about the objection. Sure, they're saying why they don't want your product. But if you're ever going to sell them, you need to uncover all such negatives and deal with them. The absolute worst thing that can happen to you in a selling situation is to have prospects just sit there, mute with blank stares. You don't know what they're thinking or what they're concerned about. You have no idea of how to direct your selling presentation. With objections, you uncover issues of concern to your prospects and identify those points you must address to close the sale. Sure, you'd like to have them tell you your product is great and how it will satisfy their needs. That's a closing cue. Salespeople alert enough to recognize closing cues hop right on them as an opportunity to begin negotiating final terms and conditions. Thing is, though, you seldom get closing cues early in your presentation and you will *never* get a closing cue if the prospect is harboring unanswered objections. Early in the presentation you get objections. Handle them effectively if you want closing cues down the road. Listening through the prospects' objections does more than identify negative perceptions about your product. Listening also helps you uncover *all* their points of concern: the benefits they're looking for; their hot button. Make a quick response to an objection and you could miss out on information that can help you isolate those features and benefits which could close the sale later in the presentation.

When you hear an objection, then, resist the urge to interrupt your prospect with an immediate answer. Instead, first listen, then feed back the objection with a reflective statement to confirm understanding, such as

"You're saying, then, that price and reliability are most important to your office..."

"So you're concerned that this model might be outmoded six months down the road..."

"Then you believe our price is too high..."

"You feel you just don't have adequate space…"

"You think, then, that the competition gives you everything you need…"

If the prospect responds with "Yes, that's correct," good. You've isolated the objection. Should they answer with "Well, not exactly," good again. You've identified a point on which you don't fully understand their position. Ask for a clarification to confirm understanding.

Encourage the prospect to talk. Listen. Isolate, clarify, confirm. Then, disarm your customer. No, I don't mean frisk the person for concealed weapons. I *do* mean to remove any negative attitudes and feelings. Objections are negative customer statements. As such, they may tend to be argumentative and confrontational. At the very least, since the prospect is giving you reasons why your product is unsuitable, there may be a tendency for the development of a negative emotional climate. And customers—who are never wrong—never buy under the cloud of a negative emotional climate. Therefore, having clarified the objection, it's important that you follow that up with a disarming statement in which you agree with your prospect that the point raised is a good one. Don't get me wrong. That does *not* mean that you should agree with the objection. It *does* mean that you convey that the points of concern are reasonable. Something like:

"I can understand your feelings…"

"That's an interesting observation…"

"You've brought up a good point…"

"I see why that would concern you…"

The disarming phrase takes away any negative edge, and enables you to maintain a positive adult dialogue. At this stage, you may have a complete and thorough understanding of the objection. But maybe not. If not, ask the customer to elaborate further:

"How did you happen to arrive at that conclusion?"

"What is it that makes you feel that way?"

"It seems to me you have a strong reason for saying that. Would you mind telling me what that is?"

Remember, at this point you are only attempting to have the prospect state and clarify the objection and the reason behind it. Continue to listen, but do not answer the objection. In fact, urge the prospect to provide you with even more reasons for not buying from you:

"Is there anything else you're concerned about?"

"Are there any other points you feel would have to be addressed?"

"Can you think of other factors that are particularly strong for the competition?"

This approach may seem a bit familiar. It is. As in any negotiation—and dealing with objections is negotiation—you want to identify all relevant variables and get the complete shopping list before you tie the package together. The amateur salesperson considers objections an obstacle to be knocked out of the way as quickly as possible. The amateur salesperson either hides from objections or attempts to sidestep them when they are raised. Unfortunately, objections are like a minefield. If you don't locate, uncover, and remove them, they'll blow you away. That's why the professional salesperson encourages the prospect to air objections. Once they're all on the table, the professional salesperson knows what has to be done to achieve agreement. You must address those reservations to the prospect's satisfaction. There are three other points to consider here about objections.

# (1) Anticipating the Customer's Objections Should Be Part of Your Pre-approach Preparation

Put yourself in the customers' shoes. Don't just think of features/benefits which will make them want to buy. Also think of all the reasons they won't want to buy—known as objections—and prepare a response when, not if, the point is raised. I'm sure you've been in an interpersonal encounter when the other party said something and, 30 seconds later, you thought up the perfect response. It would have been just right at that moment, but was useless 30 seconds later. It's the same with objections. When it's *time* to answer, you'd better *have* an answer. Thirty seconds too late and you may be lying dead in a minefield. Certainly you can't anticipate every possible objection; but if you'll think about it, I'm sure you can come up with nine out of ten. Take the time to do so and have an appropriate response at your fingertips.

# (2) Seek Out the Reason Behind the Objection

Is it really an objection or a tactic designed to intimidate you into making a unilateral concession? Is it really an objection or an indication that the customer doesn't have all the facts and needs more information? Just what are the real needs behind the prospect's objection and stated position? Is this an OBjection—something holding the customer back which can be identified and dealt with—or a REjection—a definitive "No" to your product, your company, or you?

# (3) Don't Create Unnecessary Objections

Often, customers make statements which appear to be negative in tone but are not obstacles to the sale. Don't turn them into objections by treating them as objections. Take, for example, the old Volkswagen Beetle. A prospect in the showroom might comment that it was ugly. Not a real objection. No need for the salesperson to address design aesthetics. Ignore it with a "It'll look beautiful every time you make a car payment," or "...when you fill the tank every week for three bucks." Be alert for comparable non-objections in whatever you sell.

Similarly, don't create unnecessary objections by failing to close on cue. The window of customer receptivity opens only briefly. Miss the buying signals, the window closes, and you're mired in objections for which you only have yourself to blame. Like this:

> A:  Take a look at our new model.
>
> B:  Wow, it's beautiful.
>
> A:  And it's priced at only $22,000.
>
> B:  That's cheap at twice the price. Can I get it in black?
>
> A:  Sure. Black, yellow, red, and fuchsia.
>
> B:  Oh boy! I've got cash today. Do you have a black one in stock? Can I drive it home tonight?

A:   Certainly. We have one right over there, and we
     have four more black ones coming in next week.

B:   Really? Maybe I'd better wait and look at them.

A:   No need to do that. They're all equipped the
     same.

B:   But the one you have might have a bad paint job
     or something.

A:   Not at all. Just look. It's perfect, isn't it?

B:   Yeah, it looks OK.

A:   So, let's go inside and sign the contract.

B:   I'm not sure. I'd like to see those other ones first.

A:   But this one is perfect. See for yourself.

B:   Yeah, but I've got to think about it. Gotta go now.
     I'll be back next week. I promise.

Listen to your prospect and encourage objections, of course. But remember that your objective is to close the sale. When the customer indicates acceptance of your proposal, terms, and conditions, close then and there! Otherwise, your opportunity is gone and you may be permanently spinning your wheels in the minefield of objections.

# Secret 2:
# Classify the Objection as Content or Relationship

An objection is an objection is an objection, right? Wrong! Objections come in two very distinctive forms, fundamentally different from each other. And there are fundamentally different tactics for handling the respective forms of objections.

We just saw the importance of encouraging the prospect to air his or her objections. Listen carefully. Use a disarming phrase. That helps establish positive adult–adult, two-way communication. But then, before formulating a response, you must first classify the objection.

Objections are classified according to two of the dimensions of communication in Chapter Three: content and relationship. A *valid* objection is content based. The reasoning behind a valid objection is logical and factual, *as the customer perceives the facts to be*. An important point to remember is that the customer's facts may be in error, unsubstantiated, or based on rumor or innuendo. No difference. It's still a valid objection if the prospect believes there may be a content-based problem.

The other classification is the *visceral* objection, which is relationship based. The reasoning underlying a visceral objection is emotional, not logical or factual, and generally concealed by the prospect. For example, the customer may simply not care for you because you're too young or too old; are a woman or not a woman; have long hair or hair too short. Why should that make any difference? Well, it shouldn't, but since when do human beings act logically and rationally?

Visceral objections may arise because of a negative attitude toward your company. A left-wing environmental radical may associate your company with pollution or the military–industrial complex. You may represent Ford Aerospace and all the customer can think of is that damn Pinto she used to own.

You can get hit with visceral objections if your prospect lacks buying authority but is reluctant to admit it. The result? You get one "No" after another rather than an admission that he or she isn't empowered to make a decision.

Visceral objections are often called excuses, smokescreens, or red herrings. They sound logical but are really emotional. And often, prospects even come to believe the visceral objections are factual. Customers may say, "We're fully satisfied with your competition." But in reality they're just set in their ways, averse to change, or reluctant to make a decision. They may not really be satisfied but have come to believe they are since it lets them avoid having to do something. Yes, there are people like that out there.

Since valid and visceral objections are so different, and it's essential to classify the objection before answering, you'd like me to give you a simple method for classifying objections, right? I wish it were that easy. Unfortunately, most visceral objections come disguised as valid objections. People usually won't say they don't like you because you're too short, don't like your company because it's located in a Republican congressional district, or just don't feel like making any decisions today. And so, initially, you should take an objection as valid. However, if you begin getting a series of objections, one after another, you should start to ask yourself whether the real objection is visceral and relationship based. As an example, let me cite a typical scenario I'm sure has happened to you at some time in your personal life. You meet a "prospect" in town Saturday night and call them up on Monday. This happens:

| | |
|---|---|
| You: | Hi, this is Hal Holweet. |
| Prospect: | Who? |
| You: | Hal Holweet. I met you at Trader's Saturday night. |
| Prospect: | Oh, yeah. You. |
| You: | Say, I was thinking that maybe we could get together tonight. |
| Prospect: | No, I'm afraid not. I've got an exam tomorrow morning. I have to study. |
| You: | Oh. Well, how about tomorrow night? |
| Prospect: | No, I can't. I have choir practice. |
| You: | Well, maybe I could join you at choir practice. I love to sing. |
| Prospect: | No, that wouldn't be possible. The director won't let us bring guests. |
| You: | Then how about Wednesday? |
| Prospect: | Wish I could, but I have a class Wednesday night. |
| You: | How's Thursday look? |
| Prospect: | I'm sorry, but I just don't plan that far ahead. |

Do you get the idea? The customer raises an objection. You answer with a possible solution. There is another objection; solution; another objection; and on and on. A few of these and you should begin to surmise that no matter what you say or do, you're going to get hit with another objection. The real problem isn't factual content, it's visceral relationship. And no amount of facts or logic will turn around an emotional visceral objection.

It isn't easy to pinpoint visceral objections. But if you find yourself going around and around, spinning your wheels but getting nowhere, ask yourself: Could it just be that I'm trying to use logic and facts, when the issue is really visceral and relationship?

# Secret 3:
# Break Away from Visceral Objections

One word for dealing with visceral objections: Don't. Don't deal with visceral objections any more than you have to. They're negative and they're relationship based. That means no win. If your instincts tell you that you're getting visceral objections, that's your cue to shift the conversation away from relationship and redirect it to facts and content.

Often, visceral objections arise out of customer complaints or a failure to follow up a sale by you or your company. That's why, in the opening phase of your presentation, you should touch base with the customer to be sure there are no loose ends that need to be tied up. An unhappy customer is a guaranteed source of visceral objections, so first things first. Don't assume that dissatisfactions will disappear as long as you don't bring them up. They won't. Ask the customer if they're completely satisfied or whether any points need to be addressed. If they're less than happy, good. Deal with the issues head-on and determine what actions you need to take. Dissatisfaction is relationship based. By shifting the conversation to specific actions and activities, now you're talking about facts and content. You avoid visceral objections by focusing on actions which will eliminate negative feelings. Get those feelings out in the open and determine what you'll do.

It may be very easy, or profoundly difficult, to shift away from visceral objections and move the discussion toward facts and content. It all depends on the intensity of the prospect's emotions. If those emotions are very mild, you might just ignore the objection completely. On the other hand, if the emotions are intense, it may be necessary to discuss those feelings before moving on. Remember, though: Don't bog yourself down in the quagmire of visceral objections. Deal with them only as much as is necessary, and then shift to facts and content.

For example, let's say you're a sales rep for the *National Blabber*, a weekly tabloid specializing in revealing all the personal secrets of the stars and reporting the latest Elvis sightings. You've just made a presentation to a grocery store manager, attempting to place a *National Blabber* rack at every checkout. You summarize and the customer responds:

>You:     So, if you placed a *National Blabber* rack at all your
>          checkouts, you'd sell about 200 copies a week and
>          make over $80 in extra profit.
>Customer:  You mean people actually read this trash?

Classify the objection. First of all, it is not valid, since it is not based on facts and logic. Therefore, it must be visceral. Or is it? Yes, it's an expression of feelings, but is it really an objection? I don't think so. It's really just a statement of astonishment, not something holding the customer back. It does not require you to address the literary merits of the *National Blabber* or any other facts about its content. Ignore the statement and move on.

>You:     They sure do. Especially the kinds of upper-
>          income shoppers in this store. Here's where I think
>          you ought to place the racks. Does this look good
>          to you, or would you want to get them up a little
>          closer?

Notice what happened in the example. You completed your presentation with a summary statement. The customer's response was neither a rejection nor an objection. That means one thing: Close! Don't get sidetracked on the irrelevant. All you'll do is create unnecessary objections.

Let's look at another example. You represent the Washington Watchband Company and are attempting to persuade the manager of a shopping mall boutique to carry your line. This happens:

>Customer:  I don't believe I'm interested. There's just no
>          market for a product like that in this store. I've
>          never carried watchbands and none of my
>          customers have ever asked for them.

Classify the objection. Here are the facts: The store has never carried them, and customers have never asked. Are these valid objections? No! Yes, facts were cited, but do these facts represent a logical basis for the conclusion? No, they don't. The objection is visceral, based on the preconceived opinions of the prospect. But what if the customer had said:

>Customer:  I don't believe I'm interested. There's just no
>          market for a product like that in this store. A store
>          like this one, at the other end of the mall, took on

a similar line a few months ago and they never
sold a one.

That's a valid objection—a factual basis for the opinion. But let's go
back to the former situation, a visceral objection. We can't just ignore it
and move on. And, of course, the customer is never wrong. So, how do
we move away from this negative attitude and shift the conversation to
facts and content? Here are two techniques:

**Technique 1—The Barber Chair.**    Be careful with this one. It's a little
hokey and contrived. But you can adapt it to your own style, the customer, and the situation. If you prefer, use an ice cream dispenser or hot
dogs and sauerkraut. It goes like this:

> You:    Tell me something. How many haircuts a week do
> you do in this store?
>
> Customer:    Haircuts??? Are you out of your mind? This is a
> fashion boutique, not a barber shop!
>
> You:    You're right. But if you put a barber chair there, I'll
> bet you could do some haircuts in this store.

Do you catch the drift? If it's not there, no one buys it and no one
asks for it. If it *is* there, you get sales.

**Technique 2—Feel/Felt/Found.**    This is the classic technique for shifting out of visceral objections and into facts:

> You:    I know how you *feel*. Many of our customers *felt*
> the same way. But they *found* that their sales
> average was over $100 a week.

With this technique, the "feel" is a disarming statement. The "felt"
statement acknowledges that you understand their feelings and that
their reaction is consistent with others. And the "found" statement is a
success story from those others which shifts the discussion to facts and
content.

Feel/Felt/Found is effective as long as you don't keep repeating the
words feel, felt, and found. You don't want to say "feel" and have your
customer think "Good grief. Here comes the 'felt' and the 'found.'" Mix
it up: "That's a good point. In fact, just last month a boutique manager
told me that. But we put them in her store, and...." Or: "I can under-

stand how you might think that. I'd say as many as half our customers had reservations at first. But let me show you these sales figures...." It's the Feel/Felt/Found technique, but it can be done without the exact words.

For another example with visceral objections, let's consider a situation in which the objections arise due to the customer's relationship with your competitor. Say you're a real estate agent representing Riverside Realty, calling on a prospect with the objective of listing her house:

> You: Hello, I'm Sue Sanderson of Riverside Realty. I notice you have your home for sale by owner. Tell me, have you sold it yet?
>
> Customer: No, we haven't, but we're not interested in talking to any agents. We're going to try to sell it ourselves.
>
> You: That's fine. I may be able to provide you with some information which will be useful to you. It will only take about 20 minutes. Is now a convenient time, or would tomorrow be better for you?
>
> Customer: You're just wasting your time. If we don't sell it on our own, we're going to list with Portage Properties.
>
> You: Oh, really? Any particular reason for selecting Portage?
>
> Customer: Yes, they're well established and very professional. And one of their agents goes to our church.
>
> You: I know several agents who work for Portage. They're very good. Who is it that you know?
>
> Customer: Wendy Widebotham.
>
> You: I don't believe I know her.
>
> Customer: She only works part-time. We play bingo at the church every Friday night.

Hold it right there. The customer says she's selecting your competitor because they're established and professional and she already has an agent. So what do you do? Do you overcome the objection by demonstrating that you and your company are better established and more professional? That's the logical and factual way, isn't it? Yes it is, but logic and facts won't win since the objection is visceral: The prospect has a friend in the business and she feels obligated.

You don't want to deal with the visceral objection, and you surely don't want to tell the prospect she's wrong to choose an agent based on friendship. What you must do is guide the prospect to focus on logic and facts. That's first. Then do your presentation. How? There is no set way, but analogies are often useful:

> You: If you needed to have some dental work done or some legal documents drawn up or some renovations done on your home, and you had a friend who worked part-time as a dentist or lawyer or contractor, would you go ahead and hire that person or would you consider checking out anyone else?
>
> Customer: I guess I'd check around.
>
> You: What sort of things would be important to you in making a decision?

Then move from the analogy and ask what things are important in the sale of a home. For those items they don't volunteer, ask:

> You: Would the selling price be important? Would the time it took to sell concern you? How about knowledge of creative financing? Or being available full-time to show the house and work with financial institutions?

You don't deal with the visceral objection. Instead, enable the prospect to become aware of factual points and their importance. Relationship becomes less of a factor; but on the other hand, the prospect has begun to develop a relationship with you and, hopefully, likes you. Now, the prospect is no longer choosing between a friend and a business professional. The prospect is choosing a friend who is a business professional.

In the business environment, you may encounter similar situations with prospects who have long-term established relationships with your competition. Generally, they'll tell you they're satisfied with things as they are. It's the quickest way to get rid of you. Again, don't bog down in relationship. Shift to content.

You:        How long have you been dealing with ABC?

Customer:   Five years.

You:        And when you made that decision, you weighed all the factors and compared them with all the competition?

Customer:   We sure did.

You:        You feel that decision paid off for you?

Customer:   Definitely.

You:        Well, then, if such an analysis paid off then, wouldn't you agree it might just pay off again five years later?

Customer:   It might.

Use the same principle if the prospect says he or she is too busy to see you. That's a smokescreen. Don't ask when they'll be a little less busy, just go for the appointment:

Customer:   I'm too busy to see you this month.

You:        That's why you need to see me. I have an idea that can save you as much as an hour a day, with no increase in cost. Can we get together this afternoon or would first thing in the morning be better?

And here's a similar situation:

Customer:   I'm too busy to see you this month.

You:        Everybody's busy nowadays. That's why I won't waste your time. Give me 30 minutes. Whether you buy from us or not, you'll get enough information to make it worthwhile. I can see you tomorrow morning, or would you prefer to meet late today?

Recall I said that generally visceral objections are concealed. Prospects will brush you off with facts and logic, though the real objection is visceral. Occasionally, however, they'll come right out with a visceral objection. You may not like hearing negative feelings about your company or you personally, but don't let it bother you. If a visceral objection is out in the open, at least you know what you're dealing with.

As long as it remains under the surface, you may not even be aware of it, let alone overcome it.

You may be able to ignore a minor visceral objection with a basic Feel/Felt/Found:

> Customer: You've only been out of college for a year. I've been in this business for 30 years. What the hell do you know?
>
> You: I see what you mean. And I know I have a lot to learn. It's interesting. One of my first customers, who has 27 years of experience, said that same thing. But just last week he told me we'd saved his company over $50,000.

On the other hand, the negative feelings may be so deeply seated that a Feel/Felt/Found is inadequate. Let's say you're a major oil company that just spilled a few million barrels in a pristine, natural surrounding. When a prospect brings that up, do you say: "I know how you feel. So-and-so felt the same way. But he found, oh, what's a little oil on the beach and a few thousand sea otters, anyhow?" That simply won't cut it. Better to respond with the consummate disarming phrase: "I'm glad you brought that up." I know you're *not* glad they brought it up, but at least it's out in the open. A successful follow-up might be: "Mistakes may have been made. We're not sure yet. Not all the facts are in. But I can tell you this: This company and its management cares about the environment. If they didn't, I wouldn't work for them. We're going to do whatever it takes to minimize the possibility of anything like this ever happening again." Just one thing: If you ever have to say anything like that, be sure you really do believe that you, the company, and its management cares. If you really don't believe it, you lack the power of commitment. Also, you lack principles.

If you or your company has made mistakes and everyone knows about them, admit your errors and move on. However, don't admit to faults if you don't have to. Here's an example:

> Customer: I don't want to hear anything about it. Three years ago I called your company and no one returned my call. Then I phoned your competitor. They had someone out here the next afternoon. I give them all our business now.

Let's just say that three years ago your company was a mess. No one cared or followed up on anything. Since then, though, you've cleaned house and now have a sharp organization. Do you say: "You're right. We were lousy then, but we're good now?" Why bring it up? Don't go beyond the prospect's phone call. There is no need to air the dirty laundry:

> You:  "I can understand your feelings, and I'm sorry that happened. But I can tell you this: That's not the kind of response you'll get in the future. I'll give you my number. If you need anything, just call me direct."

Remember that visceral objections are based on relationships, emotions, and feelings. Defuse any negative attitudes toward you or your company before getting into your presentation. And if you perceive that your prospect is influenced by a relationship with your competitor, gently shift the conversation toward points of fact. In either case, don't deal with visceral objections any more than you have to.

# Secret 4:
# Close on Valid Objections with Denial or Yield

If you've managed to shift away from visceral objections, or never had to deal with them in the first place, one thing is virtually guaranteed: You *will* have to deal with valid objections. Is this bad news? Not at all, because every valid objection is an opportunity for you to move directly into a close, and that's why objections are your friends.

You'll recall that valid objections are logical, factual, and content based. They are generally straightforward and to the point. When the prospect throws one your way, just ask yourself one question:

## Can I refute the basis of the objection?

The answer to that question determines your choice between the two techniques for handling valid objections.

**Technique 1—Denial.**   You use this technique to deny—or refute—the objection by introducing new facts or by presenting the facts in a different light. Be careful, though, not to prove the customer wrong. Instead, after a disarming phrase, help them to see how they can be even more right.

Here's our first example. You're selling widgets and the prospect raises a price objection.

| | |
|---|---|
| Customer: | We can't go with that price. |
| You: | I can see why price would concern you, but I believe we're competitive on every line. |
| Customer: | Amalgamated has you beat. |
| You: | They do? |
| Customer: | Yeah. Their price is $24. You quoted me $27. |
| You: | What kind of quantity were they talking about for that price? |
| Customer: | 10,000 units. |
| You: | I see what happened, then. We've been talking about 1,000 units. If you were interested in 10,000, our price would be $24 as well. Will you be needing 10,000? |
| Customer: | If I can save $3 a unit, I'll take 10,000. |
| You: | How soon will you want delivery? |

In this first example, the customer raised a valid objection—price—which you were able to refute by bringing in new facts. Having done so, close! Here the close was attempted with two assumptive closes, inquiring *how many* would be needed and *when* they wanted delivery.

Here's our second example. You're selling corporate jet aircraft. Again, you encounter a price objection.

| | |
|---|---|
| Customer: | How much is this plane? |
| You: | It's complete and ready to fly for $3 million. |
| Customer: | Way too high. We can get a Gooney 2CV for $2.5 million. |
| You: | Are you concerned about the price? |
| Customer: | Of course we are. We have to go with the low bid. |
| You: | Is it the *lowest* bid or the *best* bid you're looking for? |

| Customer: | I'm not sure I follow you. |
|---|---|
| You: | Here's what I mean. The *best* bid is determined by the total operating cost of this aircraft over its lifetime, of which initial price is only one element. Generally, the lower the initial price, the higher the costs for fuel and maintenance, and the lower the reliability. If you're in an aircraft at 35,000 feet, I'm not sure you want to compromise on reliability at any price. And, you should consider what it'll be worth three, five, or ten years down the road when you replace it. Those things are important, aren't they? |
| Customer: | Certainly. |
| You: | On that basis, then, wouldn't you agree that total cost is the all-important factor, not just the initial purchase price? |
| Customer: | That seems reasonable. |
| You: | Then let me show you how this aircraft will give you superior service and reliability, at less total cost, over its lifetime. |

In this example, you refute the valid price objection by presenting the facts in a different light. Having persuaded the prospect to focus on long-term cost rather than solely the purchase price, you move into a close by demonstrating your cost advantage.

And finally, here is our third example. Classify the following objection.

| Suburban parent: | I never let my kids eat at McDonald's. I heard somewhere they have worms in their hamburgers. |
|---|---|

Visceral objection, you say, based on a negative attitude toward the company specifically or fast food in general? It can't be valid, can it? Everyone knows McDonald's uses 100 percent USDA-inspected beef, no fillers, no worms. But no, if the parent is expressing true feelings, this statement must be classified as a valid objection. Sure, the facts are in error. Sure, they're based on hearsay, rumor, or innuendo. But nevertheless, if this parent believes there may be a product problem, this objection should be treated as valid and addressed with denial.

You may think it's incredible that anyone would actually believe

McDonald's had worms in their hamburgers, but it actually happened. Remember the wormburger scare, to which McDonald's responded with an ad campaign emphasizing their use of 100 percent pure beef?

Though totally unfounded, such rumors may seem believable to their customers, particularly in the midst of related news reports such as the recent beef contamination and poisoning deaths experienced by a competing chain.

You may also think it's pretty incredible that anyone would believe that your product causes cancer or that your compressors have been known to spontaneously explode. But incredible or not, if information from *any* source raises a content-based objection by your prospect, don't just laugh it off as unbelievable. Deal with it as a valid objection and provide your prospect specific facts to refute it. Then ask a closing question:

> You:   "So, as you can see, the United States government certifies our burgers are 100 percent pure beef. That's the kind of quality you want for your family, isn't it?"

When faced with a valid objection, your first choice is to use Denial. That is, you hope you can refute the objection with new facts or by putting the facts in a different light. Sometimes, though, they've got you. The prospect raises a valid objection which is a legitimate reason for not buying and which you can't refute. In such a circumstance, you must employ:

**Technique 2—Yield.**   Make a disarming statement and then yield to their point. Yes, that *would* be a good reason not to buy or that *would* be a good reason to buy from the competition. After all, what else can you do? It *is* the truth.

The key to the Yield technique is that you quickly acknowledge the customer's objection and then immediately move on to cite compensating benefits which more than offset the reason not to buy. Yes, you must *quickly* acknowledge and move on. The longer you get hung up on a legitimate reason for not buying, the less the likelihood you'll ever get the sale. Immediately agree that the customer has raised one good reason not to buy; follow up with three, four, or five reasons why the customer *should* buy, and then ask him or her to confirm agreement that the positives outweigh the negatives.

The Yield technique is identical to the Ben Franklin balance sheet close, which will be discussed in the next chapter. On the balance sheet, there are simply more reasons to buy than not to. If the customer agrees, you've closed.

Here is our first example. You're on a job interview.

> Customer:  I see that your grade-point average is only a 2.3.
>
> You:  That's right. And that's not as high as I'd like it to be. But I've had to work 50 hours a week to get through school, and I've been actively involved in university and community organizations. Last year, I was Employee of the Month twice on my job and received the mayor's award for good citizenship. I believe that demonstrates I'm an achiever, wouldn't you agree?

And for our second example, you sell manufacturing equipment.

> Customer:  I can get the same machine, including a service contract, from your competitor for $50,000 less.
>
> You:  You're right, we do cost more. But we've been working together for five years and you know we're reliable. Also, you can get service from us seven days a week, 24 hours a day, not just Monday through Friday from 9:00 to 5:00. And we have a complete inventory of parts here, not in Kansas City. So, when you consider everything, our proposal is a good investment, isn't it?

Remember the two basic techniques for handling valid objections: Denial if you can refute the objection, Yield if you can't. In either case, your answer should move you directly into a close.

Here are a few variations. Let's say you sell Mercedes–Benz automobiles and the following conversation occurs:

> You:  Here's one in the color you were looking for.
>
> Customer:  It's nice, but I have a tough time reconciling a price of $80,000 for a car. That's more than my wife and I paid for our house in 1975. I can get a Cadillac for half this amount.

This is a valid objection. So, should you use Denial or Yield? Well, if this were a situation similiar to our corporate jet aircraft example, you could use Denial. Let's say that in three years the Mercedes had a trade-in value of $65,000, whereas the Cadillac, bought new for $40,000, was worth only $20,000. Get the customer to focus on the three-year depreciation rather than initial price, and refute the objection by demonstrating that the Mercedes will cost only $15,000 over three years versus $20,000 for the Caddy. This one is easy.

But what if the Mercedes would be worth only $55,000 in three years? Now it costs $25,000 for three years compared to $20,000 for the Cadillac. Therefore, you might think you can't refute the objection, and thus must yield. But no! You can still use Denial, at least partially. Do that first, and then Yield. Put the facts in a different light by focusing on depreciation rather than initial price to illustrate that the difference is $5,000 over three years rather than $40,000. Quickly acknowledge that the Mercedes does cost $5,000 more, and then provide the compensating benefits. The balance sheet is more likely to tip in your favor if you can use a partial denial to minimize the "No" side of the ledger.

Another thing you can't forget: Listen! Often, an objection provides the seeds which enable you to get on the customer's wavelength and state things in terms they can relate to. Be alert! Pick up on such cues. In our example, the prospect noted that $80,000 was more than he and his wife paid for their house in 1975:

> You:    "Now, I won't ask you what that house is worth today, but I'll bet it's a lot more than you paid for it, isn't it?"

In his own words, the customer agrees that the initial price did not represent money that was spent and gone and that a long-term perspective is more appropriate. This principle is simple. If you want your prospects to see facts in a different light, help them draw from their personal experiences. Use analogies. Build agreement. Then answer the objection.

For another variation, let's say you're making a presentation to your prospect and you suggest an implementation plan. The prospect responds with a valid objection. You suggest an alternative. Another valid objection follows. Is this hopeless? No it isn't, not at all. Consider the following scenario:

> You:    About how many units do you think you'll need every month?
>
> Customer:    Around 100. But it's not that simple.
>
> You:    What do you mean?

Customer: We might not need any for as much as six or eight weeks. Then, about four times a year, a big order comes in and we need 200 right away.

You: In that case, maybe you ought to maintain an inventory of at least 200.

Customer: I haven't got the room here for more than 100. If I double my inventory, it'll cost me an extra $500 a month for warehouse space.

You: Well, then, if you need an extra 100 in a hurry, we could air freight them out and you'd have them the next day.

Customer: Yeah, but air freight would cost us an additional $25 a unit.

It doesn't look very good, does it? There is a valid objection to maintaining a sufficient inventory: warehousing costs of $500 a month. And there is a valid objection to air freight: a per unit cost of $25 for an extra 100 units four times a year. It looks like there is no way to win; or is there?

In the next chapter, we'll discuss closing as a process of building agreement. And one of the most effective closing methods is getting the customer to discuss *how*, not *if*, they're going to buy. Note your first statement in the example: "About how many units do you think you'll need every month?" That's a closing question. When the customer answers ("Around 100"), it's an indication that you've reached agreement in principle and must now iron out terms and conditions. The objections which follow are not objections to your product. They are points of concern about alternatives for implementation. Therefore, since you've already reached agreement in principle, don't get bogged down with unnecessary objections. Instead, continue to close by focusing on *which* alternative is best. First, ask the customer whether there are additional alternatives to the first two, of more warehouse space or air freight. Then, get them to choose among the alternatives. In this example, more warehouse space will cost $500 a month or $6,000 a year. Air freight will cost $25 a unit multiplied by a hundred units four times yearly, or $10,000 a year. Unless there's another alternative, it looks like extra warehouse space is the way to go. In closing, that's called a choice technique, and hopefully the customer will continue toward final agreement by choosing *how* to implement the purchase. But this may not happen. He or she may just come back with "Yeah, warehousing is the least expensive, but it's still an extra $6,000." This is a valid objection and you can't deny it. You have to yield: "You're right, it'll mean an investment in warehousing. But when you consider this benefit and that benefit and this benefit, it's still a good decision, isn't it?"

# Secret 5: Move On with Your Presentation After Objections

There is one last area to cover on objections. By now, I hope you've come to agree that objections are your friends. They give you an opportunity to discover points of concern for your prospects and enable you to uncover their hot buttons and buying motives. And valid objections help you move directly into a close with either a Denial or Yield technique. Having dealt with an objection, you know more about your customer and what it will take to close the sale. But having dealt with an objection, there's one thing to do: Move on. Don't let the objection sidetrack you. Get your presentation back on course toward achieving agreement. If you fail to take the initiative, it's most likely that the momentum of your presentation will be lost. Let objections help steer your course, but don't let them derail you. Keep your call objectives in mind and move on.

# Summing Up

This chapter has addressed the Five Top Secrets of Overcoming Objections. Let's review them:

- **Secret 1:** Listen. Resist the temptation to answer immediately. An objection is an opportunity to get your prospect to talk. And if you listen, you may learn what you need to know to close the sale.

- **Secret 2:** Classify the objection. Determine whether it's a relationship-based visceral objection or a content-based valid objection. That's important since the respective types must be handled differently.

- **Secret 3:** Break away from visceral objections. They're negative and emotional, so don't deal with them any more than you have to. Defuse the negative feelings and shift the discussion to facts and content.

- **Secret 4:** Move from a valid objection directly into a close through Denial or Yield.

- **Secret 5:** Move on after answering an objection. Don't let objections take you off course. Keep your presentation on track toward a successful conclusion.

Wow, we're almost done! Don't put this book down now, because in the final chapter we're going to tie all the loose ends together where the rubber meets the road: Closing the sale.

# Closing Is the Final Boost

## The Four Top Secrets of Closing the Sale

We have arrived at the final chapter. And the critical point to remember here is that if you can't close effectively, all the previous seven chapters are for naught.

Here's an analogy. Think of a selling situation as a shot across the Grand Canyon in a rocket sled. The first seven chapters give you seven–eighths of the fuel you need to get across. This final chapter, on closing, provides the final boost to propel you safely over to the other side and the attainment of your objective. If you had no fuel at all you'd simply spring out of the catapult, fall over the edge of the cliff, and crash to the canyon floor below. But if you had seven–eighths of the necessary fuel, you'd make a good takeoff, soar for a while in a perfect trajectory, but then sputter out short of your goal. The result? There is no difference. You still crash to the canyon floor.

On a rocket sled, seven–eighths of the necessary fuel is no better than no fuel at all. In selling, a perfect presentation will be totally ineffective if you don't know how and when to close. There's just no such thing as seven–eighths of a sale.

In this chapter you'll discover the Four Top Secrets of Closing the Sale that will give you one last little boost toward your objective. First, you need to know when to start closing and understand what motivates people to buy. Then, understand how to ask a sequence of closing questions and how to employ closing techniques in a professional manner. And finally, after your presentation, be sure to critique the call and make plans for service, follow-up, or another call.

# Secret 1:
# Know When to Start Closing

You begin closing the moment you meet your prospect face-to-face—the very first moment. Then, throughout your meeting, never lose sight of the ABCs of professional selling. ABC stands for:

## Always be Closing. *Always.*

Recall the point about closing that was made in Chapter Six. Closing is a process, not an isolated event. You may think of "the close" as a direct request for action: Do you want the blue one or the red one? When would be the most convenient time for delivery? Will this be cash or charge? And yes, that final question, asking the prospect to buy, is the culmination of the closing process. But it's merely the frosting on the cake, and you've got to bake that cake before you can frost it. Closing is the total process of getting all those ingredients together, mixing them in the proper proportions in just the right sequence, and baking the mixture at the prescribed temperature for the appropriate time. Applying the frosting is simply the final step before you get to enjoy the end product of your total effort.

And if you need to negotiate terms and conditions, "the close" represents only an agreement in principle. Depending on how well you learned your lessons on power and negotiation, you'll determine whether you get to keep your whole cake, only a slice, or just a few leftover crumbs.

The process of closing is the process of building agreement in which you help prospects make decisions that will benefit them. Throughout your presentation, you build that agreement through a five-step sequence that culminates in a direct attempt to achieve the objective of the sale. Here are the five steps:

(1) Ask questions and get the prospect to talk to identify needs, problems, and buying motives.

(2) Confirm understanding with a reflective summary statement.

(3) Present features of your product and translate those features into benefits which address the prospect's attendant buying motives.

(4) Ask questions to have the customer confirm the benefits. It *may be* true if *you* say it. It *is* true if *they* say it.

(5) Make a request for action.

Let's go through an example. Here, Pat Peterson is calling on Carol Caldwell, hoping to sell her company a new line of machine tools. As you read, note how Pat employs many of the skills you've already learned about focusing on the customer, using questions, and making an effective presentation/demonstration.

> Pat:    You say you're pretty much satisfied with the equipment you're using now. What are some of the things you like most about it?
>
> Carol:    Well, it's priced competitively.

Pat:     Is there anything you'd like to see modified or improved?

Carol:   Yes. It seems we spend an awful lot of time changing drill bits. And the changeover always seems to occur in the middle of a run.

Pat:     How has that affected you?

Carol:   Well, we're averaging a little over 18 percent down time. That's high.

Pat:     How about production scheduling? Has that high down time caused you any problems there?

Carol:   On occasion.

Pat:     Really?

Carol:   Yes. Just last week we were a day late getting a shipment out.

Pat:     From what you're telling me, then, your present equipment may be costing you more than its direct cost, parts, and service.

Carol:   That's probably true.

Pat:     Then if I could show you a way to reduce that down time to 10 percent or less, that would help you, wouldn't it?

Carol:   It might.

Pat:     (handing her a brochure) Take a look at this. It's the test data comparing ordinary drill bits with ours. It shows how they last nearly twice as long in heavy-duty industrial applications. Our customers tell us they've cut their down time nearly in half. When you consider your per-unit labor costs, you'll probably save money, won't you?

Carol:   If we could get down time to 10 percent or less, yes.

Pat:     Might help on production scheduling too, wouldn't it?

Carol:   It might solve a few of our problems.

Pat:     I'm glad you agree. I was thinking that the south-west corner of Building 12 would be the ideal location for our machine. How does that sound to you?

Carol:    Overall, that's probably best. But are you sure you
          could have it completely installed by the fifteenth?

Pat:      Will you be needing it by the fifteenth?

Carol:    Yes, we will.

Notice how Pat followed the five-step sequence to build agreement
and close the sale. But did you also notice how Pat picked up on Carol's
closing cues? When she said, "It might solve a few of our problems," that
was an indication she was sold. A closing cue! That means one thing:
Close! Go directly to Step Five with a specific request for action. In this
example, Pat asked a little-decision question: Where would it be located? Also note how Pat used a reflective question to turn Carol's request
for information into a close. When she asked if the machine could be
installed by the fifteenth, he would have replied, "Yes." But what would
that have achieved for him? He would have been presenting, not closing. Remember your ABCs! With a reflective question, "Will you be
needing it by the fifteenth?" he turned a statement into a close and
caused the prospect to utter the word salespeople love the most: "Yes."

Use little decisions and reflective questions to move toward the close
whenever the customer indicates agreement, at any stage of the five-
step sequence. Little decisions are those such as how many, what color,
what size, which features, cash or charge. Get the customer making
those little decisions at the outset—saying "Yes." Move the customer
toward a close.

Compare these next two conversations:

A:    Does it come with a 5-speed?

B:    It sure does.

A:    Have you got a black one with a 5-speed?

B:    I think this one has a 5-speed.

And now this:

A:    Does it come with a 5-speed?

B:    You want a 5-speed?

A:    Yes. Have you got a black one with a 5-speed?

B:    You're in luck. This one just came in. If it hasn't
      been sold yet, have you got a $500 deposit so I can
      hold it for you until we process the paperwork?

Another way to get the prospect saying "Yes" is to place a tag-on at the end of a sentence to turn a statement into a question. Some examples...

Don't say:  This model is rated tops by *Consumer Reports*.

Do say:  This model is rated tops by *Consumer Reports*. That says a lot about its quality, doesn't it?

Don't say:  This policy insures your home for replacement cost.

Do say:  This policy insures your home for replacement cost. That's real peace of mind, isn't it?

Similarly, use a tag-on in response to a customer question and get him or her to confirm the benefit:

Customer:  What kind of mileage does it get?

You:  It gets 35 miles a gallon. That'll save you a lot on gas, won't it?

And this:

Customer:  How much will it cost to print out a page?

You:  About 50¢. Sure is less than having your secretary type it, wouldn't you say?

Another variation of this, called the escalator technique, asks questions to confirm benefits *before* identifying the respective features. You use the escalator when you suspect the prospect might not be willing to hear you out if you identified your product or company up front. Insurance salespeople and direct selling representatives regularly use this technique, and we all know why. What's your visceral reaction when someone tells you he or she represents an insurance company? Quick exit, of course. So instead, a salesperson could run the prospect up the escalator:

You:  I guess you, like most people, would agree that nothing's more important than the safety and financial security of your family, wouldn't you say?

Customer:  I'd say so.

You:  A lot of people nowadays seem to feel they can't depend on the government to take care of all their needs. What do you think about that?

| Customer: | You gotta be crazy if you depend on the government for *anything*. |
|---|---|
| You: | So, wouldn't you agree that it makes sense to have a personal financial goal and a plan to get there? |
| Customer: | Sure, but right now I can barely pay the bills every month. |
| You: | I guess that's true for everyone. Would you say that one reason for that is all the taxes you're paying? |
| Customer: | That's the truth. |
| You: | Then, if I could show you a way that over the next 20 years you could save an average of $3,000 a year in taxes, invest that money with no taxes on the interest, and at the end of that time have over $137,000 in cash, would you want to hear about it? |
| Customer: | I sure would. |

With the escalator, you ask questions about benefits for which you feel confident of receiving an affirmative response to build agreement. Just be careful and don't ask them in a manner which is offensive and calls for an obvious answer, such as, "You love your family, don't you?"

In the last chapter, you'll recall that every time you encounter a valid objection, your answer should lead you directly into a close. And in a negotiation, where you've already reached agreement in principle, always be closing as you iron out the specific terms and conditions. Whenever you make a proposal, or suggest a trade of concessions, follow up with a closing question to confirm agreement on your terms.

Above all, be alert for closing cues. Don't get so wound up making your presentation that you miss them.

# Remember: Your objective is to close the sale, not to complete the presentation.

If and when the prospect indicates agreement, ask for the order then and there. And don't expect the prospect to say something like "Gee, you sold me. Where do I sign?" Generally, closing cues are subtle and nonverbal. They can be a change of posture, a nod of the head, the tapping of a pencil, leaning back, leaning forward, eyes looking up, eyes looking down, faster speech, slower speech—some change in their over-all communication pattern.

If you're fully prepared for your sales presentation, you won't be stumbling along trying to think of what to say next or attempting to extricate yourself from a hole you've dug yourself into. You'll be able to focus on the customer and pick up on the body language that tells you it's time to close. When you sense a cue that indicates agreement, go for it!

When in doubt, close. If you're unsure and hesitate for even a second, the moment is gone and the opportunity may be lost forever. Understand that one thing holds you back: Fear. You may be afraid of failure or afraid you might offend your prospect by asking a closing question. We've already discussed fear of failure. And as far as the prospect goes, you're more likely to offend by not asking for the order when that prospect's ready to buy than by asking when they're not ready. At the worst, you'll get an objection, and as you know, objections are your friends.

When do you close? From the very beginning.

# Secret 2:
# People Are Motivated to Buy When They Feel the Opportunity to Buy May Be Lost

By now, you already know that people don't want features, they want benefits. And *which* benefits they *really* want is another matter and it's based on basic human nature.

No one wants what they know they can have.
People only want something they believe they
might not be able to get.

This truism is not limited to the selling environment. It extends to all human endeavors.

Remember the first love of your early adolescence? What happened when you expressed your endearing affection and said you didn't need or wish to date anyone else, and wished only to worship at your beloved's feet? You probably got a "Gee, that's nice," with all sorts of logical reasons, which you now recognize as visceral objections, as to why the two of you ought to see a variety of other people and perhaps be just "friends."

By the time you graduated from high school, it's likely you'd discovered that an expression of undying love was a sure ticket to oblivion for you. The flip side of the coin was that you had no trouble attracting people you didn't want.

Hopefully, those painful lessons of your youth taught you one of the prime principles of human behavior: No one wants what they know they can get, but people are motivated to buy when they feel their opportunity to do so may be lost.

It's a basic human characteristic that people want the best, and the best deal, they can get. If they know they can get something today, and they know the same deal will be there tomorrow, they have no incentive to make a deal today. Tomorrow a better deal may come along.

You may know you're the best person that special someone could ever find. In selling, you may know you have the best product at the best price. But no one is going to want you or your product unless they feel they may lose out if they don't act right away. It's simple. No one wants what they know they can have, but people will fight for something they fear they might not be able to get.

It makes no difference what you sell. You may be selling yourself to a potential spouse or employer. You may be selling a product or service to a potential client. In selling anything, you *must* create competition for your offering. You *must* convey to the prospect that the opportunity may be gone forever if he or she lets you walk out that door today. And you *must* be prepared to turn around and take that walk if the prospect won't meet your bottom line terms and conditions.

I do not like to rely on "techniques" to close a sale, but I do urge you to employ this one, albeit tactfully. I've heard it called the "standing room only" close, "impending event," or "special feature." Whatever you call it, it's a reason why the prospect must buy today or lose out. Car dealers are famous for this one. Have you ever gone shopping for cars and *not* had the salesperson tell you that the one you're looking at would be gone later that day because a couple was coming in to buy it for their son? And real estate agents always say you'd better put in a contract today, because another couple has looked at this place three times and is ready to make an offer. Why do they do that? They do it to create competition for what they're selling. Why do they do that? They create it to make you think you might lose out if you don't act now. Why do they do that? They do it because it works!

In your pre-approach preparation, always think of reasons why your prospect must buy now. Supplies are running short; there's a price increase tomorrow; the special promotion ends today; someone else wants it; the order must be processed today or we can't guarantee delivery. If you can't think of a reason, make one up. Perhaps there will be a Teamsters' strike or a nuclear war.

The one thing you can be sure of is that if you can't provide your prospects some compelling reason to buy today, they probably won't buy today. Why should they, if there might just be a better deal coming down the road tomorrow? That belief virtually guarantees smokescreens and visceral objections of "needing time to think it over." Learn a lesson from your youth. Convey to your prospect that if they don't take advantage of the opportunity today it will be gone.

# Secret 3: Know How and When to Close the Sale

Having just said that I'm not too crazy about closing techniques, let me present a few more. But also let me reemphasize the importance of not over-relying on techniques or using them in an improper context. By now, you should appreciate the fact that closing is the process of focusing on the customer and building agreement throughout the presentation. On the other hand, there are points in your presentation when you need to stop presenting and make a direct attempt to achieve the objectives of the sale. In other words, close!

By a direct attempt I do not mean hitting the prospect between the eyes with, "Well, that's my presentation. How about it? Can I have your order?" First off, that's a "Say No" question. You never ask a closing question that can be answered yes or no. And most important, it's just too direct. A close should be a gentle nudge which moves prospects from feeling positive about your product to negotiating the specific terms and conditions of how they'll buy your product.

Finally, keep in mind that on an average it will take you at least five attempts to successfully close the sale. By that, I do not mean you will get shot down four times before you finally hit the target. I *do* mean that you will go through five closing scenarios, each one building agreement a little bit more, before you'll achieve agreement in principle. As we've noted, you must be alert at all times for closing cues. Whenever the prospect indicates that he or she is sold, go into a closing scenario. If the scenario results in agreement in principle, your presentation is over and you get down to terms and conditions. If agreement is not reached, continue along, ever alert for the next buying signal.

Let me present two situations under which a closing scenario should be attempted and two—and *only* two—techniques appropriate to each situation:

# The customer appears "sold" and conveys a cue indicating a willingness and readiness to buy

Remember: The cue may be a direct statement like "That does look nice" or a subtle nonverbal cue such as a pause or a nod of the head. In this situation, the cue should turn on a red light in your gut which says "Go for it." Use one of the following techniques:

**Technique: Assumptive Close.**    As its name would indicate, with an assumptive close, you make a statement or ask a question which assumes the prospect will buy. If their response maintains the continuity of your conversation, the sale is closed. Generally, you'll do an assumptive close in the form of a secondary question. Here are some examples:

> You:  So you can see how this equipment can give you better reliability in the long run.
>
> Customer:  Hmm, it might at that.
>
> You:  The assembly section would probably be the best location. Do you already have a 220-volt line in that area?

|  Customer: | Yes, we've got 220 capability throughout the plant. |
|---|---|
| You: | Good. Would it be more convenient for you if we installed it over the weekend? |

Or this:

|  You: | How does the coat feel? |
|---|---|
| Customer: | Very good. |
| You: | It looks nice, too. Are you going to be needing some new ties to go with it? |

In your pre-approach preparation, think of several secondary questions you might use as an assumptive close:

- "Will delivery by the fifteenth be soon enough?"
- "Would you like me to gift wrap that for you?"
- "What budget code will be assigned to this shipment?"
- "Would you care to go ahead and order your appetizer now?"

**Technique: The Choice Technique.**    Similar to the assumptive close, this technique presumes the prospect will buy. But instead of asking a secondary question, it asks them to choose among alternatives of *how*, not *if*, they'll buy. This technique is particularly appropriate early in the presentation as you guide the prospect in making little decisions. Again, some examples:

|  You: | This model comes in red, white, or blue. Which one do you think would fit in best with the decor of your patio? |
|---|---|
| Customer: | I think the red one. |
| You: | Good. We can deliver it tomorrow, or would you prefer to take it with you today? |

Or this:

|  You: | The basic model is $1,000, but for just $200 more you get a bigger engine and an electric starter. That means it'll last longer and you'll never again have to go through the aggravation of pull- |
|---|---|

starting. What do you think? Will the basic one do the job for you or do you think the deluxe model is worth a little more investment?

Customer:    I hate pull-starting.

You:    I know what you mean. Will that be cash, check, or charge?

As with assumptive secondary questions, think of several choices you can ask the prospect to make in the course of the presentation:

- "Will 100 cases be enough, or do you think we ought to go with 150?"

- "Would Friday be a good time, or is Monday a better day for you?"

- "Do you prefer Aisle 7 or Aisle 9?"

- "Do you want blackwalls or raised white letters?"

The first situation, where the customer sends you a cue that he or she is ready to buy, is the easy one. The other closing situation is a little tougher:

# The customer appears "sold" and is expressing no objections

However, he or she seems unwilling or not ready to make a buying decision. Naturally, I trust that you have already conveyed a rationale for buying today since the opportunity may be gone tomorrow. And I assume you're not spinning your wheels on visceral objections.

Your objective in this situation is two-fold:

(1)  Uncover and handle any valid objections holding them back.

(2)  Get them to make a decision now.

Use one of the following techniques:

**Technique: The Ben Franklin Balance Sheet.**    Be very careful how you use this one. I will describe it in its pure form. A salesperson says to the prospect, "I know it's a tough decision, but here's the way old Ben Franklin would go about deciding something." Then the salesperson takes out a piece of paper, writes "Yes" at the top of the left side and

"No" at the top of the right side. Next he or she reiterates all the benefits raised in the presentation and all the reasons to buy today, listing them under "Yes." Turning to the prospect, the salesperson asks, "Can you think of any reason *not* to buy." There are two possibilities:

(1) The buyer says, "Gee, no, I can't." The salesperson comes back with an assumptive close or a choice technique and wraps up the sale.

(2) The buyer says, "Yes, I can." The salesperson has uncovered the objection.

The salesperson can refute the objection with a valid objection Denial if the objection can be refuted, or if it cannot be refuted, employs a valid objection Yield by noting it under the "No" column, and then says, "So, in balance, wouldn't you say the decision is yes?" Obviously it is since the salesperson has stacked the deck with a plethora of yesses. The prospect agrees the "Yes" side outweighs the "No" side, and the salesperson nails it down with an assumptive choice. It sounds easy and it is easy—and it's effective. But, as I said, be careful.

The reason I urge caution with the Ben Franklin is because it's got to be the world's oldest closing technique. In fact, Ben himself may have invented it. The last thing in the world you want to have happen is for the prospect to say or think, "Good grief. I can't believe it. He's doing the Ben Franklin Balance Sheet. I haven't seen that in years. Wow! I can't wait to tell everyone at lunch."

This technique is old. In its pure form, it's hokey. Therefore, I urge you not to mention Ben by name or draw the line down the middle with the Yes and No on each side. Instead, just take a pad and write down the reasons to buy as you review them with your customer. When you're done, ask the prospect if there are any reasons not to buy. If there are none, close. If there are any, deal with the objection. Use this same approach on "buy today" versus "wait until later." If you've done your homework, you should have good reasons why the prospect should buy and should buy today. The reasons not to buy or to wait until later are objections. And, as you know, objections are your friends because every objection moves you directly into a close.

A variation of the Ben Franklin is the summary close. This is the same technique, only it's done orally rather than on paper. Do either one or both as it fits your style. The only way either one will fail is if the prospect's "No's" outweigh your "Yesses" or the prospect's "wait until later" outweighs your "buy today." If that's the case, you don't get the sale. And if that's the case, you don't deserve the sale.

**Technique: Eliminate the Negative.**    This technique has the same objective as the Ben Franklin: Uncover an objection or persuade the prospect to make a buying decision now. But its style is different. Instead of you stating the positives and letting the prospect supply the negatives, with the eliminate-the-negative technique, *you* volunteer potential reasons for them *not* buying and then you either eliminate that reason or confirm it as an objection. Like this:

> You:    It's not the price, is it? You've seen how we can match or beat anyone.
>
> Customer:    No, your price is OK.
>
> You:    Is there any problem with system compatibility?
>
> Customer:    No, I don't see any.
>
> You:    Anything on parts, service, or warranty?
>
> Customer:    No, they all look pretty good.
>
> You:    Do you have any questions about the integrity and reliability of my company?

In theory, by eliminating any possible reason not to buy, the customer will finally see the light and agree to close. In practice, I have a basic problem with this technique: I don't like dwelling on negatives. And with eliminating the negative, you run the risk of pointing out a potential reason for not buying which hadn't occurred to the prospect until you brought it up. Like the thought, "Hmm. Integrity and reliability of the company. Wasn't I just reading...." Therefore, I'd tend to recommend the Ben Franklin or summary close as a first step. If, then, you still haven't uncovered an objection but can't get them to budge, you might give the eliminate-the-negative technique a shot before bailing out completely. If you're not getting anywhere by that point, chances are you're dealing with a visceral objection. Return to Chapter Seven.

With all these techniques in hand, let's go on a sales call with Steve Swanson, a sales representative for the Mobility Systems Company. Today he is calling on Harry Hoffman at Clark Courier Service, a small firm specializing in the delivery of legal documents for attorneys and their clients. Steve has just entered Harry's office.

> Steve:    How are ya doing, Harry? I'm Steve Swanson of Mobility Systems Company.
>
> Harry:    Nice meeting you, Steve.
>
> Steve:    (handing Harry a pamphlet) This is what I was

telling you about on the phone: the Dynamo 99. It's a complete cellular phone system, fax machine, and duplicating machine all in one. It's just what you need for every vehicle in your fleet. Like having an office on wheels.

Harry:   It looks big.

Steve:   Not big at all, considering what it'll do. Not much larger than a window unit air conditioner.

Harry:   But our fleet cars are Nissan Sentras. It would never fit unless we took out the front seat on the passenger's side.

Steve:   That'd handle it. Take a gander at page three, Harry. You can have the Dynamo 99 for just $3,599.

Harry:   $3,599? That's about half what we pay for the car.

Steve:   Yeah, but you'll never have to fill the Dynamo 99 with gas, and it'll never have a flat tire.

Harry:   I'm afraid it's just more than we could consider right now.

Steve:   (taking a calculator out of his briefcase) Let's see what we can do. How many vehicles do you have in the fleet, Harry?

Harry:   Five.

Steve:   (punching in some numbers on the calculator) My boss won't like this, but I'll tell you what I'm going to do just for you. If you'll sign a contract today for five systems, I'll sacrifice them for $3,299 each.

Harry:   Steve, we're just getting this business started. We simply don't have that kind of money.

Steve:   You sure are a tough negotiator, Harry. OK, I'm at your mercy. Make me an offer. Will you give me three grand?

Harry:   Three thousand, three million, it's all the same. We can't do it.

Steve:   Harry, we will not be undersold. Show me the best competitive deal and we'll beat it. What kind of equipment do you have in the fleet now?

Harry:   We don't have anything.

Steve:   Not even a beeper, a two-way radio, or a cellular phone?

Harry:   No.

Steve:   What do you do? Send your guys out every morning with a bag of quarters?

Harry:   No, we just have them call in whenever they make a pick-up or delivery.

Steve:   And it doesn't cost you anything?

Harry:   No. Except in unusual circumstances or when they break for lunch. Then they'll use a pay phone. But that only happens two or three times a day for each person.

Steve:   Sure would be nice to have a fax machine and a duplicating machine at their fingertips when they're on the road, though, wouldn't it?

Harry:   I can't say. We've never really needed them. We only transport originals of legal documents.

Steve:   Then you're in for a pleasant surprise. Once you've had fax and duplicating machines in your fleet, you'll wonder how you ever lived without them. It's like a microwave oven.

Harry:   Like a what?

Steve:   A microwave oven. Do you have one at home?

Harry:   Yes, we do.

Steve:   And now that you have one, would you ever have a home without one?

Harry:   I can't say. My wife does all the cooking.

Steve:   Let me tell you, Harry, you'll love 'em.

Harry:   I don't know. I'll have to think this over.

Steve:   Think it over? What's there to think over? We've got the best product, the best price. And I won't be able to give you the same deal tomorrow. Can you think of any reason *not* to buy today?

Harry:   I'm just not going to make any decisions today.

Steve:   No problem. Tell you what. I'll leave this offer

open until Monday. What if I call you then?

Harry:    Monday will be fine.

Steve:    Well, take it easy over the weekend, Harry. I'll talk to you on Monday.

So, how would you rate Steve's presentation on a scale of 1 to 10? Certainly, he remembered his ABCs, employing assumptive, choice, special feature, and Ben Franklin techniques. You can't fault him about being too shy to ask for the order. Of course, he did commit one of negotiation's deadly sins by making a unilateral concession on the price.

It's likely that intuitively you rated Steve's performance as very poor. He was obnoxious and overbearing, the stereotypical image of a "salesperson." But hopefully, by now, you can critique his performance and identify his specific mistakes. Perhaps you've never been as inept and offensive as Steve, though I suspect we've all been guilty of some of the things he did. Let's review his performance and touch upon some of the highlights covered in this book.

To begin with, Steve's focus was entirely on his product and himself instead of the prospect and the prospect's needs. He talked features, not benefits, and he talked too much. Steve didn't employ effective questioning techniques and he didn't listen. He viewed closing in isolation rather than a process of building agreement. Without a foundation of rapport and agreement, his closing techniques were ineffective. And he attempted to ramrod through Harry's objections rather than making them his friends.

How could he have done things differently? Let's look at a parallel case, as Barb Boyd calls on Kay Kaufman. As you read, take note of all the points we've covered throughout these eight chapters.

Barb:    Good morning, Ms. Kaufman. I'm Barb Boyd from Mobility Systems Company.

Kay:    Kay Kaufman. Good to meet you, Barb.

Barb:    You're new in this office, aren't you?

Kay:    Yes, we are. We've been open for about three months.

Barb:    Are you just getting started, or is this just a new location for you?

Kay:    We're just starting out. My partner and I each worked in a legal services firm for five years. We felt there was a need for a courier service to serve the legal profession, so we decided to give it a shot.

Barb:  Do you work exclusively within the legal profession?

Kay:  Yes, we do. Attorneys and their clients, as well as judges, prosecutors, and the local, state, and federal administrative officials.

Barb:  Interesting. So what would you say is the most important benefit you offer to prospective clients?

Kay:  I'd say it comes down to professionalism and reliability. We know the legal system and the process of expediting documents. The legal profession runs on paperwork and the serving, filing, and registering of documents.

Barb:  Would you say that timing and efficiency are important to you?

Kay:  No doubt about it. We always hear our clients telling us stories about what's happened when a document was filed 15 minutes late.

Barb:  Well, Kay, I believe I have some ideas which may help you in your business.

Kay:  How can you do that?

Barb:  Just by answering a few questions. First of all, in your fleet of cars do you have any sort of two-way radio or cellular phone system?

Kay:  No, we don't.

Barb:  Do you ever have to reach your couriers when they're out on the road?

Kay:  Every once in a while.

Barb:  How do you do that if you have no way to contact them?

Kay:  We have them call in whenever they make a pick-up or delivery, so we usually hear from them once or twice an hour.

Barb:  What if you have to get hold of them between deliveries?

Kay:  That doesn't happen very often.

Barb:   About how often would that happen?

Kay:    Oh, maybe once or twice a day.

Barb:   Has that ever caused you any inconvenience?

Kay:    Every once in a while.

Barb:   Really?

Kay:    Yes, a couple of days ago we just missed a courier after a delivery.

Barb:   Hmm…

Kay:    He was halfway across town before he called in. Then he had to backtrack to a block from where he'd been.

Barb:   Do your couriers ever have a problem finding a phone to call in on?

Kay:    That's seldom a problem. All our deliveries are to business offices. They just phone in from there.

Barb:   And this involves no cost to you?

Kay:    Almost none. Maybe two or three times a day, like when they break for lunch, they'll use a pay phone. That runs us less than $20 a week for everyone.

Barb:   If your couriers had a fax machine in their vehicle, how many times a day would they use it?

Kay:    They wouldn't. We only transport original documents. If someone wanted to fax something, they'd do it themselves. They wouldn't need us.

Barb:   So you'd say your couriers require nothing more than the ability to communicate with your office by phone.

Kay:    That's correct.

Barb:   And overall, how satisfied are you with the way you're handling that communication now?

Kay:    I guess it's pretty good.

Barb:   Is there anything in particular that you especially like about the way you're doing things now?

Kay:    Well, the price is right.

Barb:   You were telling me that sometimes you miss

contacting your couriers when you need to. Is there anything else which you feel is an inconvenience or which you feel could be improved?

Kay:    I guess you'd have to say that sometimes it seems to take forever for them to call in.

Barb:    I'll bet that's annoying.

Kay:    It certainly is.

Barb:    (handing Kay a pamphlet) Kay, I believe your firm should consider the Dynamo 22 cellular phone and paging system. The phone fits conveniently in any car. And when you call, if they don't pick up after three rings, the system activates a beeper which notifies them to call in. That means they always get your message immediately, whether they're in the car, on a call, or breaking for lunch. That would address some of those points you were telling me about, wouldn't it?

Kay:    It might at that.

Barb:    This system is available on either a lease or purchase plan. On a two-year lease the total investment is just $107 per week for each system.

Kay:    That's over 20 times what it's costing us now!

Barb:    In direct costs, yes. But from what you were telling me, wouldn't you say it's costing you that much or more in lost business and added expenses by not having instantaneous access to your couriers at any time of day?

Kay:    I'm not sure it's costing us $107 a week per courier.

Barb:    Yes, but as you were saying, professionalism, reliability, and efficiency are your most important services. These systems will improve those services, won't they?

Kay:    You may have a point. How long would they take to install them?

Barb:    About an hour each. Would some time during the week be good, or would the weekend be better?

Kay:    We need all the cars during the week.

Barb:    Then we'll schedule installation for Saturday. If you'll just initial this agreement, I'll phone in the work order from my car. I believe you're going to be very satisfied with the Dynamo 22.

Kay:    Sure will be nice not having to sit around here waiting for that damn phone to ring to get a hold of those guys.

The difference is like night and day. Barb knows the top secrets of selling. Barb is a professional salesperson. Focus on the customer. Ask questions. Get *them* to say it. Build agreement. Close on cue.

# Secret 4:
# What to Do After the Close

Yes, there is life after the close. Let's consider the two possible circumstances, and a few points for each.

## The Close Was a Success

You got the order and ironed out all the terms and conditions. There are now two things you need to do:

**(1) Reassure the customer.**    You know that funny feeling you get in the pit of your stomach when you've just initialed the agreement. You think to yourself, "Good lord, I just bought a British sports car. Wonder if it'll be raining the first time it breaks down and I'm standing by the side of the road with the hood up." Psychologists call this "buyer's remorse." So, reassure your customer with a quick one-liner like, "I'm sure you'll really enjoy this on your vacation." This first step should take no longer than 3.5 seconds. Then,

**(2) Depart quickly.**    Yes, get out of there. Don't hang around discussing the stock market or the Academy Award nominations, because the longer you linger, the more likely it is your prospect will think of an objection which hadn't occurred to him or her until then. If that happens, your sale just got unclosed, and you're back to your presentation. So much for your plans for that commission check you just calculated in your head.

# No Sale

I hate to say it, but even though you're now a Kimball-trained salesperson, you're not going to be successful on every sales call. No one is. When this happens, learn from the experience. First of all, thank the prospect for his or her time. Leave the door open for a follow-up call. They may not be ready to buy today, but perhaps in a month, perhaps in a year, or even later, they may be ready. Let the prospect know you'll keep in touch and be back.

Then, as soon as you get back to your car—and before your next call or next anything—critique the call:

- What did you learn that you didn't know before?

- What did you do well?

- What could have been improved?

Make plans for a follow-up call:

- A thank-you note in three days

- An informational mailing in three weeks

- A call for an appointment two weeks after that

No, you didn't get that sale today, but with your new knowledge and a new plan, you've improved your prospects for the next assault.

And, of course, never forget what you must do between calls: Service, follow-up, service, follow-up, service, follow-up! Don't let your customers think that the only time they hear from you is when you're looking for an order. Remember: You can't *not* communicate.

# Summing Up

In this chapter, we've uncovered the Four Top Secrets of Closing the Sale. Let's review them:

- **Secret 1:** Know when to start closing. You begin to close from the very beginning of your presentation by building and confirming agreement. Always be closing.

- **Secret 2:** Know what people really want. No one wants what he or she can have. You must create competition for whatever you possess and a sense of urgency for making a decision today.

- **Secret 3:** Know when and how to close the sale. Just remember, though, not to use techniques in isolation. Closing is a process, not isolated tactics.

- **Secret 4:** Don't stop after the close. If you got the order, don't skimp on service and follow-up. If you weren't successful, learn from the experience and come back, come back, and come back.

# A Final Word

I wrote this book because I believed it would provide the reader useful information. For you, the next step is to put this information to work. Take some time to plan and set priorities. Ask yourself what you really want to do and chart a course for getting there. Learn to focus on other people. Listen to them and discover what they want and need. Achieve what you want by helping them get what they want.

Review the skills of asking questions, negotiating, overcoming objections, and closing. Plan and rehearse using these skills for every presentation you make, whether it's to one person or one hundred people.

I sincerely hope this book will help you reach your goals and dreams, both professionally and personally. Good luck and good selling.

Bob Kimball
Pensacola, Florida

# Index

# American Marketing Association

———

As a marketing professional or student you'll never get enough information about marketing.

One way to stay up-to-date with the latest academic theories, the war stories, the global techniques, and the leading technologies is to become a member of the American Marketing Association.

For a free membership information kit
phone: 312-648-0536,
FAX: 312-993-7542,
or write to the American Marketing Association at 250 S. Wacker Drive, Chicago, Illinois, 60606.